CROWD-
SOURCING

CROWD-SOURCING

AIRBNB, KICKSTARTER, UBER AND THE DISTRIBUTED ECONOMY

LIGHTNING
GUIDES

> "More people in more places can now compete, connect, and collaborate with equal power and equal tools than ever before."

—THOMAS L. FRIEDMAN

Widely hailed as the fastest-growing startup of all time, Uber has fundamentally changed the way we think about logistics. Anyone with a car, a smartphone, and a few minutes of free time can reap the benefits of employment from one of the world's largest transportation companies. And Uber is not alone. With Airbnb, anyone with a free couch can operate a hotel within their home. A campaign on Kickstarter can fund a venture and turn an idea into a business. Lending Club has democratized loans, and Indiegogo has fundamentally changed charitable giving. What we are seeing, across the globe, is democratizing of supply and demand, of labor and consumption, of investment and entrepreneurship. This leveling of the playing field is reshaping whole industries, with consumers, creators and suppliers all benefitting. It is a virtuous cycle, enabled by technology, that is reshaping our ideas about work, travel, manufacturing, distribution, and finance.

CONTENTS

INTRODUCTION

hether you know it or not, you're part of a crowd. And a crowd can be very useful.

Crowdsourcing—the process of completing a task by inviting the general public to help—has been around since the early 1700s, when the British Parliament offered a prize to whoever could create a standard longitudinal measure. Crowdfunding—asking each person in a large crowd to make a small donation—dates back to the same time, when the Irish Loan Fund was established to provide small loans to low-income Irish families.

The Internet has made it much easier for companies to take advantage of the activities of a crowd. Think of YouTube, which invites everyone to upload and share their personal videos; or Threadless, a T-shirt retailer that prints user-supplied designs; or Flickr, the immensely popular photo-sharing website and online community.

These days, the participation of a crowd can make or break a billion-dollar company. However, the democratizing effects of the internet mean that big companies aren't the only ones who can use crowds to their advantage. So can you. With a simple service like Kickstarter or Patreon, you can harness the actions of a crowd to fund your own feature film, start a new charity, or even become the next YouTube star.

Everyone belongs to the crowd, and anyone can lead it. Knowing how to use the crowd—and how the crowd is using you—is potentially the most powerful skill at your disposal.

TOYOTA
CROWDSOURCED ITS
1st insignia in 1936

1885
THE **FIRST** KNOWN
application of
CROWDFUNDING
was the
STATUE OF LIBERTY
PEDESTAL

THE EDELMAN TRUST BAROMETER
NAMED ENGAGEMENT & INTEGRITY
2 ATTRIBUTES THAT MOST
BUILD TRUST IN BUSINESS

2013
"CROWDSOURCING"
was formally added
to the dictionary.

What are some best practices for crowdsourcing?

One of the best ways to engage users is to create a community around your project. Allow people to make their own avatars, and give feedback on completed work. This allows users to feel appreciated, making them feel a part of a large endeavor as opposed to being responsible for a small task.

Who is the "crowd"?

The "crowd" refers to a variety of resource needs. These needs include users with personal interest in the project or business, access to materials needed, skills, and experience.

What are the risks of opening projects to the public?

In making projects public, you run the risk of users unintentionally contributing bad data, or submitting the wrong answers to your problem. In order to avoid these issues, it is a good idea to build your project in a way that allows you to validate submitted data.

What type of work can be crowdsourced?

Nonspecialized tasks, also known as microwork, are best suited for crowdsourcing. You can pay professionals for their expertise and experience, and outsource small tasks and simple work. Crowdsourcing complex projects only makes sense when the skills and expertise required are distributed among the users.

Who is involved in a crowdsourcing project?

The main players in a crowdsourcing project are the companies, individuals, or organizations with a task that needs to be crowdsourced. The users, or individual participants providing solutions (and sometimes intermediaries such as websites or mobile platforms), enable the process.

What are some crowdsourcing intermediaries or platforms?

A variety of websites and platforms are available. For research and development, some top sites are InnoCentive (innocentive.com), Innoget (innoget.com), and One Billion Minds (onebillionminds.com). For marketing and design, some well-known platforms are CMNTY (cmnty.com), crowdSPRING (crowdspring.com), and OpenIDEO (openideo.com/challenge).

How does crowdfunding relate to crowdsourcing?

Crowdfunding is a type of crowdsourcing. It is the practice of funding a project or business venture by asking large groups of people or communities for small donations.

How much can be raised by crowdfunding projects?

Star Citizen, a combat video game from the designer of Wing Commander, raised $76.1 million on Kickstarter even though the campaign target was $500,000. Pebble Time, a smartwatch venture, raised $19.1 million on Kickstarter. Ethereum, a decentralized publishing platform, raised $18.4 million in bitcoins. There is no limit as to how much one can raise, but there are of course thousands of people who never reach their goal, and therefore never see a dime.

WHAT'S WHAT?
CROWDSOURCING VS. CROWDFUNDING

GET TO KNOW WHAT YOU NEED

CROWDSOURCING

Crowdsourcing is an all-encompassing term that defines any act of reaching out to communities of people on the Internet for project support. This support can take the form of ideas, feedback, labor (either specialized or nonspecialized), or solutions for a problem.

These problems can be broken down into smaller parts, called microtasks. Microtasks are small, well-defined jobs that can be performed independently. They require some human participation or intelligence, versus tasks that can be automated with computers, but are not so overly complicated that they require specialization.

As such, microtasks can then be proposed to the crowd through an open call on the Internet and then completed by users on the web for a small payment.

Websites such as Amazon's Mechanical Turk (mturk.com), Clickworker (clickworker.com), and Samasource (samasource.org) host microtasks on marketplaces where Internet users can sign up and complete these jobs.

Examples of these kinds of jobs include: assigning keyword tags to images, entering receipt data, and classifying paragraphs for a legal topic, all of which pay up to 75 cents per completed task.

Being able to outsource work to the crowd has huge benefits for companies, allowing them to save on expenses for employees they would otherwise have to hire to do small, sometimes sporadic work.

An added advantage for companies is having access to a flexible workforce that can complete tasks in a short amount of time, as Internet users are positioned all over the world in different time zones.

Workers can also increase the amount of crowdsourcing they engage in, based on the project needs at hand.

PULITZER PRIZE

Pulitzer raised $100,000 in six months in 1884 to pay for the pedestal of the Statue of Liberty. That's $2.4 million in 2015's money. The average donation from a single person was $1, about $24.39 today.

Businesses no longer have to worry about creating consistent workflows or hiring additional in-house staff when small tasks are outsourced. This increases cost-effectiveness by reducing recruiting and training expenses associated with hiring new employees and paying hourly wages. It also reduces overhead costs such as taxes, paid time off, and employee benefits. By paying for outsourced tasks rather than employees' time, companies increase the value of every cent they spend.

Finally, crowdsourcing allows businesses to try new projects without incurring greater financial risk. Want to find out if you have a viable product? Get input from the crowd! Want to market a new line and see if there is consumer interest? Make it available to the crowd as a beta version, and get real feedback on the product, plus free marketing in the form of word of mouth and increased user interest.

Crowdsourcing is hugely beneficial for businesses that rely on consumer interest, have small repetitive tasks that need to be completed, or need to bring down their overhead tasks by outsourcing work.

CROWDFUNDING

The first known application of crowdfunding dates back to 1884, when, after the American Committee ran out of funds, Joseph Pulitzer of the *New York World* urged the American public to donate toward the construction of the Statue of Liberty's pedestal. Pledging to print the name of every contributor no matter how small the amount given, Pulitzer inspired the pride and imagination of a generation of New Yorkers, raising over $100,000 in six months from more than 125,000 donors, each of whom donated an average of $1 or less. The pedestal was completed in April 1886.

More than a century later, in 1997, fans of British rock group Marillion—without any involvement from the band—started an Internet campaign to underwrite the group's entire US tour. They raised $60,000 in donations collected online, inspiring the band to use this method of funding to finance, record, and market its next four studio albums.

Four years later, in 2001, the first fan-funding website, ArtistShare (artistshare.com), was founded by musician and computer programmer Brian Camelio. Building on the principles of Internet open calls and recognizing the need for an alternative business model in an industry plagued by Internet piracy, Camelio set out to offer fans an experience that could not be freely shared over peer-to-peer networks, nor downloaded from torrent websites. Offering users the chance to witness their favorite artists' creative processes, be named as a supporter on an album, or enjoy a private concert, ArtistShare is a highly successful rewards-based platform whose projects have won nine Grammy Awards and 18 Grammy nominations since its first fully funded project in 2003.

Thanks to the unbridled success of ArtistShare, crowdfunding sites started to appear with ever increasing rapidity after 2003. EquityNet (equitynet.com), Pledgie (pledgie.com), SellaBand (sellaband.com), Indiegogo (indiegogo.com), and GiveForward (giveforward.com) were all started within five years of Artist-Share's first project success.

REWARDS-BASED FUNDING

The most popular and widely known form of crowdfunding is the rewards-based model. This model encourages the distribution of an incentive, typically a product or service, in exchange for a donation. Websites such as ArtistShare, Kickstarter, and Indiegogo are all great examples. Such websites typically host projects that fund the arts, social-justice campaigns, and entrepreneurs and small businesses.

Since its inception in 2009, more than $1.6 billion has been pledged toward projects on Kickstarter. The platform boasts more than 8 million backers and more than 2 million repeat backers for a total of over 21 million individual pledges.

Of over 200,000 launched projects, about 37 percent have been successfully funded, and 10 percent raised $10,000 or more. The top categories on Kickstarter are film and video, which, when combined, represent almost half of all successfully funded projects.

Sites like Kickstarter and Indiegogo are intermediaries that connect campaigners with backers, enabling the two parties to determine the success of individual campaigns and projects. Still, users and financial backers assume risks. There is no guarantee that project developers will fulfill their rewards programs, let alone fulfill them within their time constraints, although intentional fraud is quite low. A 2013 study from the University of Pennsylvania found that less than 1 percent of Kickstarter funds go to projects that have little intention of delivering results.

DONATION-BASED FUNDING

Charities and religious organizations were collecting donations long before crowdfunding appeared on the Web. However, sites such as GoFundMe (gofundme.com), YouCaring (youcaring.com), and GiveForward (giveforward.com) now allow individuals to appeal to the online crowd for funds to pay for medical expenses, funeral expenses, or memorial funds.

GoFundMe, the pioneer of donation-based crowdfunding, has raised over $850 million in 350 campaigns from 10 million donors in the five years since its founding in 2010. The site, like many of its type, charges a 5 percent fee on funds to cover operating expenses such as payroll and technology infrastructure, and for its services as a major provider of Internet traffic and financial support.

Created in 2013 after the Boston Marathon bombings, the Bucks for Bauman campaign is the single most highly funded project on GoFundMe to date. It raised over $800,000 for survivor Jeff Bauman, who lost both legs in the tragedy.

DEBT-BASED FUNDING

Since the financial crisis of 2008–2009, credit for small borrowers has declined, making peer-to-peer (P2P) lending a viable source for small loans.

Debt-based crowdfunding lets individual borrowers apply for

unsecured loans, and if approved by the intermediary platform or site, the borrowers secure loans from users and then pay them back with interest. P2P platforms collect revenue by taking a percentage of the loan amount from the borrower and a loan-servicing fee from investors.

Most P2P platform services, such as application reviews, credit checks, and loan disbursements are automated, making the process cheaper and quicker for borrowers than traditional banking services. Interest rates are high enough to create strong returns for individual investors and are potentially better than traditional money markets and bonds due to the low approval rate from most sites.

Lending Club (lendingclub.com), the largest P2P network in the world, has an approval rate of about 10 percent. Each borrower whose application is approved receives a credit-risk score and interest rate set by the respective P2P platform. Investors can choose borrowers based on their risk profiles and reason for wanting the loan. In all instances, the risk for investors is that the borrower will default on the loan, in which case some or all of the investor's capital may be lost.

As of December 2014, Lending Club issued more than $7 billion in loans, over 50 percent of which was for refinancing, followed by 20 percent for credit card payoff and 22 percent for all other categories.

EQUITY FUNDING

Inspired by the rise of crowdfunding sites online, capital-raising professionals now offer their services over the Internet through equity-offering platforms. Their services include matching startups with investors, disclosing deal terms, and facilitating investments.

Governed by the Regulation D Securities Act of 1933, these platforms allow issuers to raise unlimited amounts of capital in each offering or campaign, though they may only do so from accredited investors. The best examples of this type of platform are MicroVentures (microventures.com), launched in 2010, and CircleUp (circleup.com), launched in 2012.

According to the Jumpstart Our Business Startups (JOBS) Act of 2012, issuers of private securities can allow up to 35 nonaccredited investors to participate in each offering as long as they do not solicit publicly (Rule 506b), or they can solicit investors publicly if they restrict themselves to accredited investors (Rule 506c). After the JOBS Act went into effect in September 2013, some equity offering platforms permitted their users to engage in general solicitation while others did not.

One disadvantage in allowing users to solicit publicly, which involves announcing and advertising the details of a securities offering to the public, is the need for investors to submit documentation verifying their accredited status each time they might want to invest, while plat-

FESTIVAL FUNDING

In 2015, thirty percent of films in South by Southwest (SXSW), a film and music festival held each year in Austin, were funded by campaigns on Kickstarter. In total, 28 films raised more than $1.7 million from over 23,000 donors.

forms that do not offer solicitation can offer investors a smoother certification process.

As of February 2015, MicroVentures had raised more than $60 million from 25,000 global investors for approximately 100 companies, making it the leading equity-based crowdfunding platform. MicroVentures and similar platforms invest primarily in seed-stage start-ups—that is, the earliest round of capital funding for a company.

TITLE III EQUITY CROWDFUNDING

Under the JOBS Act, a new form of crowdfunding platform, categorized as Title III, will be created. These platforms will allow unlimited participation from nonaccredited as well as accredited investors in the raising of capital for commercial ventures. These new platforms are awaiting the adoption of the final rules by the Securities and Exchange Commission, which is expected sometime in 2015.

These new platforms could completely transform the world of private capital, opening up a market previously accessible to only eight million accredited investors to tens of millions of potential nonaccredited investors.

Title III provisions require that all companies and business ventures participating in a Title III crowdfunding portal be based in the United States. Investment companies, such as mutual funds and private equity funds, will not be able to raise money through crowdfunding portals. There will be a cap of up to $1 million in any 12-month period, although some members of the House of Representatives have proposed an increase to $5 million.

There are also provisions for investors, including a limit of $2,000 or 5 percent of their income in equity crowdfunding investments for those whose annual income or net worth, excluding their residence, is less than $100,000. Individuals with income or net worth higher than $100,000, excluding their residence, will be able to invest up to 10 percent of their income or no more than $100,000 a year, whichever is greater.

Finally, provisions for intermediaries include a prohibition on offering investment advice or recommendations to individual investors, a requirement to register with the SEC, and registration with a national securities association.

Opinions on the new equity crowdsourcing platforms are mixed. Some analysts, such as Deborah L. Jacobs of *Forbes*, point to overregulation as an inherent problem in the proposed crowdsourcing structure. "Many observers believe there is a fundamental disconnect between the promise of crowdfunding and the system that the SEC will put in place exercising its authority," she wrote in 2013.

Others, such as Wil Schroter, chief executive of Fundable, have said that the JOBS Act will be the "single biggest event" for capital formation since the initial public offering.

"The [JOBS] Act stands to be revolutionary for many firms as well as the national economy," wrote Richard Summerfield of *Financier Worldwide* magazine. "Crowdfunding could inject much needed stimulation and job growth into the US economy."

THE TOP 10 CROWD-FUNDING SITES

1 Teespring
(teespring.com)
Established in 2011, Teespring allows campaigners to create and sell custom clothing with no up-front costs or risks. It has shipped over 6 million products to date.

2 GoFundMe
(gofundme.com)
Based in San Diego, GoFundMe has helped raise over $850 million from 10 million donors for personal campaigns. GoFundMe raises an average of $2 million daily and imposes no campaign goals or deadlines. Users keep each donation.

3 Kickstarter
(kickstarter.com)
Launched in 2009 and based in Brooklyn, New York, Kickstarter has successfully successfully funded over 80,000 projects with 8.3 million pledgers who have pledged over $1.6 billion. Known for its exciting projects and trustworthy campaigns, Kickstarter sets parameters for the projects allowed on its site and employs a dedicated integrity team that monitors suspicious activity.

4 Indiegogo

(indiegogo.com)
Established in 2008, Indiegogo boasts over 15 million visits from over 224 countries. Indiegogo offers a flexible funding model, whereby campaign creators can keep money raised even if they don't meet their campaign goals.

5 Patreon

(patreon.com) Patreon helps fans support artists they love. In its first eight months, Patreon reached just under two million page views per month.

6 YouCaring

(youcaring.com)
YouCaring is a personal funding website that is free for fund-raising organizers and campaigners. Operating entirely on the generosity of its donors, YouCaring has an average of over 3 million visitors per month and has been used to raise over $102 million.

7 CrowdRise

(crowdrise.com)
Started by actor Edward Norton (below) and producer Shauna Robertson, CrowdRise gives people the opportunity to participate in fund-raising for social causes with no goal requirements or deadlines. *Barron's* named Norton one of the Top 25 Global Philanthropists. CrowdRise was recognized as a Top Fundraising Website by Mashable.

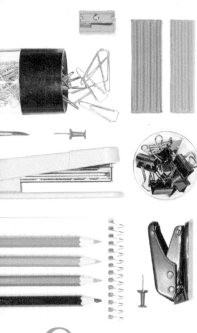

9 Kiva

(kiva.org) Kiva is a non-profit organization that links its users with individuals in need. Kiva facilitates small loans to empower people to create better lives for themselves and their families. Since 2006, more than 1.2 million lenders have financed over $690 million in loans with a repayment rate of 98.75 percent.

10 GiveForward

(giveforward.com) GiveForward is an online fund-raising and donation website that helps friends and family raise money for a loved one in need. Since its launch in 2008, GiveForward has helped raise $65 million to cover medical expenses on over 50,000 fund-raising campaigns.

8 DonorsChoose

(donorschoose.org) DonorsChoose.org is an online charity that lets users help students in need. Public school teachers across America post classroom needs on the site, and donors fund the projects that most inspire them. Started by a social studies teacher in 2000, more than 1 million supporters have funded 230,000 teachers and over 14 million students nationwide.

THE WEB MAKES A WAY

THE INTERNET AND INCREASING FREEDOMS

With the increased environmental problems and unsustainable social and economic structures attributed to the 20th century large-scale centralized industrial complex, the need for system change has become apparent.

The current economic system has largely been driven by a concept called economies of scale, under which the cost of creating a product decreases as the amount of the product made increases. This makes large-scale industrial projects a more attractive and profitable option than small-scale production.

Large industrial production has dominated mass-producing and concentrated industrial cores. Detrimental effects to individuals, societies, and the global environment have also resulted from this large-scale industrialization.

As a solution to these problems, the concept of distributed economies was born, promoting small-scale, decentralized units of production that are interconnected.

By focusing on small markets, developing unique high-quality products, and creating flexible, small-scale production systems, the notion of distributed economics stands to transform the current industrial complex into an interconnected marketplace

SoundCloud CEO Alexander Ljung

of collaboration and collective spirit.

The Internet and its inherent capacity for connection are making the way for this wave of distributed economics to flourish in the modern marketplace.

As markets become more interconnected, small businesses find new opportunities in niche markets, and specialized services satisfy the customized demands of the Internet consumer. Smaller-production operations can contribute innovative practices with market agility that bigger enterprises cannot match.

The Web is a great equalizer of companies of all sizes. When customers can find the products they desire through a Web search, the size of the firm producing that product no longer matters.

Following are three areas in which the Internet has created a way for the democratization and decentralization of industry, and where firms, large and small, use interconnectivity to innovate and create growth.

INTERNET MEDIA

Popular Internet media, such as blogs, podcasts, and self-produced videos, are all forms of decentralized media. Web users have become media contributors in networks that connect producers with audiences instantaneously, bypassing large media producers such as newspapers, television companies, and publishing houses. Before the Internet, mass media was structured as a centralized, one-way relationship where large media firms produced content that individuals passively consumed.

The power concentrated within media companies promoted bias, censorship, and uniform reporting. Interest groups, through their influence on major corporations, controlled what messaging and content was communicated through media channels.

Local Internet media outlets providing community-centered news are a popular

DID YOU KNOW

Crowdsourcing for Internet media doesn't stop at human resources. Community-sourced sites like The Lo-Down, a community website and monthly print magazine covering neighborhood news for New York's Lower East Side, also use third-party links and articles to curate targeted, audience-focused content from around the Web.

alternative to mass media companies of old. The popularity of websites such as MissionLocal (missionlocal.org) in San Francisco, MinnPost (minnpost.com) in Minneapolis, and The Lo-Down (thelodownny.com) in New York City prove that local Internet media is on the rise.

Local media offers users the opportunity to contribute by reporting news happening in their own communities in real time, which means faster and more relevant information sharing than with traditional publications, which usually print only one edition daily.

Internet news also uses fewer resources and has a lower carbon footprint than traditional models, such as newspapers and magazines, which print on paper and use cars for local distribution.

On a global scale, Internet media institutions like YouTube (youtube.com), SoundCloud (soundcloud.com), and the Independent Media Center (indymedia.org) use crowdsourcing principles to revolutionize the media market and challenge the economic model of centralized firms and one-way communication channels.

YouTube alone has helped shed light on politics, uplifted environmental concerns, and revolutionized both the entertainment and education fields by making video content instantly and

---

2.92 Million
The number of Twitter followers for Coca-Cola

40 Minutes
The time the average user spends on Facebook per day

14 Times per Day
The average number of times smartphone users check Facebook

globally accessible. SoundCloud has leveled the playing field for countless recording artists all over the world, who can now share their creations with a global audience.

EDUCATION

Internet-supported classrooms and education programs have revolutionized the way we learn. Training and education that were formerly accessible only through institutions are now decentralized and are made available to a global classroom.

Initially launched with the offering of a few online courses through existing schools, video lectures, and occasional homework assignments submitted via email, educational crowdsourcing and social media have completely transformed the way we learn.

Ninety percent of college faculty use social media in courses they teach, 93 percent of students search online rather than go to libraries, nearly 8 out of 10 faculty members report using online video for class, and more than 6 million students are taking at least one online course.

Self-directed education is also on the rise. Crowdsourced video sites such as YouTube and Vimeo (vimeo.com) host thousands of how-to videos, tutorials, and lectures on everything from tying a bow tie to advanced mathematics for engineers and everything in between.

Making education accessible to users all over the world, regardless of income, location, or perceived ability, the Internet has effectively decentralized academic institutions' stronghold on education and offered the global community a larger and decentralized market of information.

CONSUMER PRODUCTS

The Internet has become an integral part of consumers' commercial activity; 78 percent of people are using online media when researching products or services, and e-commerce sales are growing by more than 19 percent each year.

Decentralized free markets, such as NXT FreeMarket (nxtfreemarket.com) and OpenBazaar (openbazaar.org), stand to challenge and disrupt consumer product institutions' hold on consumer purchasing. They do this by offering people the opportunity to trade with one another without depending on any institution.

Using electronic contracts, called "smart contracts," to enforce agreements, wholesalers and consumers alike will be able to find each other and finalize transactions without incurring listing fees, dealing with currency exchange, or having to sign up with a website.

Decentralized markets have been a long time coming.

The fall of Napster in 2001 made many online users realize the need for secure file-sharing networks that were less prone to risk. The ensuing revolution in P2P file sharing established networks such as Gnutella, Kazaa, and Freenet, which offer user anonymity and the ability to operate without central servers. These networks operate by connecting users directly with each other to exchange information using hundreds of computers across the world working together, instead of one large central processor.

This innovation in networking led to the first decentralized financial network, Bitcoin (bitcoin.org), which was built on the principle of decentralization.

Bitcoin, a digital currency operating independently of a central bank, was established in 2009 and is used to complete

Napster's cofounder Sean Parker attends Angel Ball, hosted by Gabrielle's Angel Foundation for Cancer Research at Cipriani's on October 21, 2010 in New York City.

transactions all over the world without state regulation or credit card fees.

By eliminating consumer reliance on centralized banks and building on consumer websites that have already bypassed large companies' stronghold on the market—such as Etsy (etsy.com), eBay (ebay.com), and Storenvy (storenvy.com)—decentralized markets stand to completely revolutionize the way we do business online.

REAL-TIME MANUFACTURING

The recent emergence of digital manufacturing techniques marks the start of the third great industrial revolution and the beginning of a complete transformation in global markets.

In "A Third Industrial Revolution," published by *The Economist* in 2012, 3-D printing, robotics, and Web-based services were named the factory and production models of a new age.

Mass customization and smaller niche markets are the way of the future. Tailored product manufacturing and small-batch production are being made accessible by 3-D printing and digital design, which are doing away with the old model of large manufacturing firms and mass production. The applications of these techniques are still in their infancy, but the quality and type of products that can be printed are astounding. Hearing aids, acoustic guitars, medical models, and unique perfect-fit clothing are only the beginning of what will be possible once 3-D printers become a household item, which is the goal of many thought labs today.

Not only will household printers change the access we have to products and materials, but they will also affect how these items are made. Many manufacturing firms are already making the move away from offshore production and long-distance supply chains toward closer contact with the communities they serve. This allows them to respond more quickly to changes in demand.

For the modern innovator and small-business owner, access to large amounts of capital and huge production firms will no longer be a requirement; a laptop, Internet connection, and digital design suite will suffice.

WHAT'S NEXT?

Internet-based distributed economies signal a new age for the sustainability of society by reducing carbon footprints and improving resource and energy efficiency.

Society's transition to mobile and social commerce, driven by new technologies, will allow consumers to participate and shape their local ecosystems within a global interconnected economy.

As Internet users and consumers alike embrace social media, education, and commerce, opportunities to flourish will emerge for small and independent producers.

Web access to the global market, mobile technologies, real-time manufacturing, and virtual stores are helping level the playing field between small and large firms. Big and small companies will rely on each other to function more effectively in a global marketplace, creating a collaborative endeavor.

PRIVATE

TRANSPARENCY & REPUTATION MANAGEMENT

TRUST REIGNS SUPREME IN THE DIGITAL LANDSCAPE

Many people fear that social networking services diminish human relationships and contact, and increase social isolation. The benefits of social media, however, have been overwhelmingly positive. Social media has helped make every relationship a lasting one. We no longer lose social ties over the course of our lives; we keep Facebook friends forever—they follow us even though our paths might diverge.

Twitter has leveled the playing field between people worldwide, making one network accessible to all. It has, in turn, become the newswire for the planet. Making news and information available to everyone at the click of a button, Twitter has made broadcasters out of users, and users out of companies. Customers, citizens, and fans no longer face barriers to communication with businesses, governments, and celebrities—everyone is reachable.

"Social media is a catalyst for the advancement of everyone's rights. It's where we're reminded that we're all human and all equal," said Queen Rania of Jordan. "People can find and fight for a cause together—global or local, popular or specialized—even when there are hundreds of miles between them."

Social networking has also changed the way we conduct business.

MARKET TRANSPARENCY

While the idea of transparency in business is not a new concept, social media networks have forced both large and small firms to rethink the way they communicate with stakeholders and consumers.

Consumers now expect open access to relevant content about business structures and upcoming decisions, as well as direct lines of communication with the companies they chose to support. This has ushered in a new era of commercial business—one that relies on trust built between businesses, stakeholders, and consumers in order to fuel business growth and long-term success.

"The currency of leadership is transparency," said Howard Schultz, CEO of Starbucks. In 2015 there is no choice about whether to be transparent. Any user with access to social media can easily find information on most corporations, such as what kind of reputation those businesses have on the Internet. When McDonald's was fighting an online rumor that its Chicken McNuggets were made from "pink slime," it decided to go transparent, inviting viewers behind the scenes at a manufacturing plant to witness the supply chain for themselves. The video, which was hosted on YouTube, garnered more than 4 million views.

In 2014 Buffer (buffer.com), a social media sharing company, revealed its pay structure online in a blog post titled "Introducing Open Salaries at Buffer: Our Transparent Formula and All Individual Salaries" Applications for the company skyrocketed, and the quality of candidates improved.

TRUST

Transparency builds trust, which is very important in today's marketplace. When corporate secrets can be unraveled with a few clicks of a button or a simple Internet search, it is only a matter of time before online consumers discover the facts they need to make crucial decisions about where they invest their money.

Media reputation can tell a fuller story and have a much more powerful impact than any one tweet or Facebook post. The strongest respect is fostered for those companies that choose to openly share their process with viewers and proactively meet the demands of their customers.

In 2014 the Edelman Trust Barometer named engagement and integrity as the two attributes that most build trust in business. Engagement continues to be an area of growth for businesses, large and small. With the proliferation of Internet media channels currently at our disposal, maintaining active accounts along all fronts is proven to be the most effective model of business engagement today.

Proactive approaches that remain consistent and authentic have garnered the most respect from consumers and markets alike. Large companies like Coca-Cola and Nike lead the way.

DIVERSIFY CHANNELS

We've come a long way since Facebook launched "Pages" back in 2007 and encouraged businesses to create a presence on its social network.

Companies including Burt's Bees, Old Spice, and Threadless use Facebook to connect with fans on a one-to-one basis, promoting active discussions and product giveaways that build brand loyalty among customers.

"Facebook probably produces less than 10 percent of our sales," said Susan Webster Adams, CEO and cofounder of Candles Off Main, a Maryland retailer. "What we get from Facebook is more valuable than that. We've gained insight, support, suggestions, inspiration, and friends."

Building a reputation through online media channels means engaging with fans and potential customers, and having a consistent and proactive approach across media channels.

The key is context and timing—connecting with the right users at the right time with the right message, making a lasting impact.

On Twitter, one smart approach is to create different feeds for different aspects of business. For example, ASOS, a British online fashion and beauty retailer, has separate Twitter feeds for customer service and women's and men's fashion. This common strategy allows companies to respond to the market without getting customer-care questions mixed up with promotional messages.

> *Some of the most successful brands engage their customers by cultivating a unique voice and bringing the brand's personality to life.*

Some of the most successful brands engage their customers by cultivating a unique voice and bringing the brand's personality to life. Starbucks, for example, tweets things like "We like the color blue," and "This weekend is supposed to be amazing!" alongside promotional tweets about its diverse product line.

Social media channels can also be used to support and encourage user-led innovation, where customers help refine products and innovative markets. Theorists, such as MIT economist Eric Von Hippel, attributing online mobile banking, social networking, and the heart-lung machine to users, have proved user-led innovation is a core part of the innovative process.

Companies like Threadless, a T-shirt manufacturing site, rely on contributions from their customer base in the design process. Microsoft uses its Most Valuable Professionals program to award users who innovate and elevate Microsoft products, and Nokia uses the Concept Lounge to invite users to submit new ideas for mobile design.

Twitter has also benefited from user innovation, such as the "@reply" feature that was imported from other social networks and then adopted by Twitter after users started using it to reply to each other's messages. Another innovative user-generated tool is the hashtag, which was developed by users to organize their own messages.

Innovative users are interest-driven and work within highly active communities. The rise of social media, and the unprecedented accessibility to companies and industrial firms, prove user-led innovation to be a driving force in new markets.

MANAGEMENT

With so many different channels of communication available today, many companies turn to crowdsourcing to deliver real-time customer support and facilitate a participatory audience.

Companies like Zendesk (zendesk.com) and Crowdnetic (crowdnetic.com) provide transparency and information for global markets. Zendesk delivers cloud-based customer-service software that integrates social media accounts such as Facebook and Twitter into one interface so companies can respond to customer concerns regardless of the platform they're using.

Crowdnetic provides technology and market data for crowd-funded equities and marketplace lending equities, building on the importance of engagement and transparency in all markets today.

Additionally, digital hives, which support the active participation of company employees, are now emerging. Companies are using social media platforms to mobilize the masses and provide better customer service, formulate new strategies, and compete in flexible markets.

These digital tools help facilitate networking and collaboration among consumers, workers, and company executives. This approach makes it possible to solve problems, unlock knowledge, and speed up execution.

Connect with FACEBOOK
Why you should like this feature

1 It's important to have a verification process to ensure user identity.

2 Facebook Connect eliminates the need for multiple passwords and logins.

3 Metadata such as location, gender, and your profile picture can be carried across multiple platforms.

4 Facebook Connect also allows users to publish information to their Facebook profiles based on actions they have taken on a Connect site.

5 Every time you make a donation to your friend's Kickstarter campaign, you can publish a story on your timeline, letting everyone know that you support the campaign.

6 Facebook Connect is a tool for simplifying the website verification process, protecting the identities of online users, and making wider-reaching connections in the online world.

POTENTIALS OF PARTICIPATION

WHY SHOULD I JOIN IN?

There are now four types of sites: donations-based funding, rewards-based funding, debt funding, and equity funding. The Jumpstart Our Business Startups (JOBS) Act—signed into law by President Obama in 2012—promised to transform the crowdfunding landscape and offer greater opportunities to entrepreneurs and investors alike.

Before the JOBS Act, general solicitation—which refers to public advertising—was prohibited for early-stage companies seeking funding for new ventures. This ban was in place to protect prospective investors from fraud and misinformation. However, this ban also means that nonaccredited investors

cannot access equity funding websites, which is how most start-ups generate funds. Everyday individuals will be able to invest in private companies online and receive shares of new businesses.

ENTREPRENEURS

For people starting new businesses, looking to innovate, or even just trying to buy a new oven for their bakery, crowdfunding offers the possibility to make serious cash. There are more than 600 crowdfunding websites worldwide; in 2013 they raised more than $5.1 billion total.

The most popular form of crowdfunding is rewards based, exemplified by websites like Kickstarter and Indiegogo, where donations for projects are sought in return for nonmonetary rewards. Usually this means personalized gifts, a mention as a producer, or a free product once the project is complete.

Different websites offer different plans for funding. For example, Kickstarter runs an all-or-nothing model, where you name a fund-raising goal and only keep the funds if you meet that goal. According to its website, this helps eliminate risk. That is, you aren't responsible for completing a $5,000 project on only $1,000 in funds, and your fans are motivated to mobilize to help you reach your goal.

Other sites, such as Indiegogo, allow you to keep the pledged funds even if you don't reach your funding goal. Most sites charge a small fee from the funds once you collect—somewhere between 2.5 and 5.0 percent from a successful campaign—plus credit-card processing fees, which are usually between 2.5 and 3.0 percent.

{ **Angel investor** an investor who provides capital for a business start-up in exchange for shares }

It is also possible to use crowdfunding to acquire loans for your business project; use sites like Lending Club and Prosper, which offer instant quotes without affecting your credit score. These types of sites allow you to borrow money directly from other users, at a financing rate set by the platform, which completely eliminates the middleman banks.

These sites became hugely popular after the economic recession of 2008 significantly reduced the number of small-business loans available through traditional lending institutions.

Finally, some platforms, which fall under the category of equity-based funding, allow company shares and ownership stakes in the company to be sold to accredited investors without the traditional hurdles associated with initial public offering sales. Websites such as OfferBoard (offerboard.com), CircleUp (circleup.com), and OurCrowd (ourcrowd.com) facilitate these transactions.

Equity crowdfunding promises to be an expansive field in 2015, when the JOBS Act will finally pass through all legislative restrictions, and nonaccredited investors will have the opportunity to invest through equity-based funding.

In the past, only accredited investors sanctioned by the Securities and Exchange Commission were allowed to participate. Individuals had to have an income of more than $200,000 a year and a net worth exceeding $1 million, or they had to be a general partner or executive officer of the security being offered.

Soon, anyone will be able to contribute to a project in exchange for company shares—with some limitations. "More people will be able to get more funding in [equity crowdfunding] than they ever did before," said Slava Rubin, cofounder and CEO of Indiegogo.

INVESTORS

There are many different opportunities for investors to tap into the crowdfunding market and make good returns on their investments.

The most popular type of crowdfunding platform, the *rewards-based program*, gives investors small nonmonetary prizes for donations to different business projects and campaigns. Websites like Kickstarter and Indiegogo run this type of platform.

The incentive for investors on these platforms can be quite attractive. For example, when independent companies were just beginning to develop smart watches, investors had a chance to pre-purchase one for a set donation. Other perks are less quantifiable but by no means less important—involvement in local projects, supporting innovative ideas, and funding community efforts as its own reward.

Equity or *investment crowdfunding* offers accredited investors the opportunity to invest in start-up companies in exchange for company shares, ownership opportunities, or future returns.

Compared to rewards-based funding, where investors simply donate in exchange for a product or reward, equity crowdfunding allows them to become an investor or shareholder in a new company.

Equity crowdfunding aggregates smaller amounts of capital from individual investors who then have an equity stake in the company. While equity crowdfunding has traditionally been limited to accredited investors with certain amounts of income or personal net worth, this will change when the final rules of the JOBS legislation go into effect sometime in 2015.

Of the 8.7 million Americans who are eligible accredited investors, only about 3 percent participate in start-ups.

Drew Houston, chief executive and cofounder of Dropbox Inc., a cloud-based file-sharing application, most recently valued at $10 billion.

That's about 264,000. With the opening of the floodgates to non-accredited investors, that number is expected to triple in 2015 alone. The returns on equity crowdfunding investment can be very attractive, which is why such a large increase in investors is expected.

"While most start-ups will not achieve Facebook or Dropbox returns (62,000% and 39,000% ROI, respectively)," wrote Onevest cofounder Tanya Prive in *Forbes* magazine, "a long-term investment of five to eight years in the right start-up could produce higher returns than any other asset."

A well-balanced portfolio is diversified, and early-stage start-ups can offer assets that change in value independently of the core financial markets, providing stability and returns even if other assets decline.

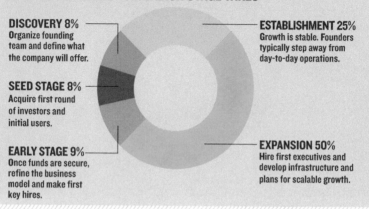

GROW TOGETHER : FIVE STAGES OF CROWDFUNDING A COMPANY, FROM DISCOVERY TO ESTABLISHMENT, AND THE PERCENTAGE OF TIME EACH STAGE TAKES

DISCOVERY 8%
Organize founding team and define what the company will offer.

SEED STAGE 8%
Acquire first round of investors and initial users.

EARLY STAGE 9%
Once funds are secure, refine the business model and make first key hires.

ESTABLISHMENT 25%
Growth is stable. Founders typically step away from day-to-day operations.

EXPANSION 50%
Hire first executives and develop infrastructure and plans for scalable growth.

The primary goal of an *angel investor*—an investor who provides capital for a business start-up in exchange for shares—is to invest early, before an idea takes off. Your best shot is to pick a start-up before they have a hit, either because they have made something great but haven't fully realized it yet, or because they are a few stages away from making a leap.

This is called the *seed stage*, which is when companies offer their ideas for funding or shares but don't have the capital to make the idea a reality. The two most important factors are the market opportunity for the idea and the team carrying it out. As an investor, it's your job to figure out whether the founders of a business have the ability to carry out their plan.

Another platform where investors stand to gain returns is *debt-based crowdfunding*, also known as peer-to-peer lending, which is where individuals can lend money to other professionals for a return in interest.

These are similar to bank loans, and applicants demonstrate their creditworthiness through checks and balances put in place by the website. Lending Club, for example, gives borrowers a grade depending on the credit score of the applicant as well as a combination of other factors, including the amount being borrowed and its intended use.

Loans are then given interest rates according to risk and volatility. Investors can choose what loan grade they wish to fund, with the higher-risk loans corresponding to higher returns and higher risk of default.

Bryce Mason of P2P-Picks (p2p-picks.com), an independent credit modeling service provider, puts a realistic expectation of returns on peer-to-peer lending at around 5 to 13 percent.

To arrive at higher rates of return on interest, you have to assess the lowest risk you can possibly take on, and diversify between higher-grade and lower-grade loans to achieve higher returns while maintaining stability.

PLATFORMS

Choosing a crowdfunding platform depends on the kind of project you're looking to invest in, what kind of incentives you're looking for, and how much public knowledge you can share.

Kickstarter, which has excellent social media outreach with over one million followers on Facebook and 976,000 on Twitter, only accepts creative projects. A campaign on Kickstarter is easy to promote, and entrepreneurs can take advantage of the platform's already-large reputation and far-reaching scope.

For investors, however, there is no existing offer for investment opportunities beyond prizes and rewards, though that might change.

Equity-based funding has been limited by the restrictions against public promotion, though that is quickly changing with the implementation of the JOBS Act. Start-ups will be able to share information about public offerings and campaign deals in 2015, and nonaccredited investors will be able to participate.

For debt-based crowdfunding, the most important knowledge for investors is already accessible through the platform site, in the form of grades given to the borrowers seeking funds.

Some of the best campaigns benefit from their founders' ability to articulate their projects in a cogent way to potential funders, showing that they have thought through how they will carry out their endeavors.

Quiz
ANALYTICS & DISTRIBUTED ECONOMY

1. Data analytics help organizations gain:
   A. Insight into customer behavior
   B. Insight into developer behavior
   C. Insight into organizational behavior
   D. All of the above

2. Which platform promises to analyze large streams of data for the financial world by offering real-time statistical computing systems and scalable analytics?
   A. Kenzo
   B. Kinko's
   C. Kensho

3. With data analytics and software, companies can get a better handle on their business.
   A. True
   B. False

4. Krowdster provides optimization tips and access to professional crowdfunding research.
   A. True
   B. False

5. Krowdster has been successful in leveraging data and insights from more than:
   A. 275,000 past projects
   B. 480,000 past projects
   C. 50,000 past projects
   D. 1,000,000 past projects

ANSWERS: D, C, A, A, B

DISPUTED DISTRIBUTIONS

ARE ALL FUNDS CREATED EQUAL?

Kickstarter enjoyed immediate coverage from the media. This helped launch its popularity and made it the face of crowdfunding early on. A few months after launch, the *New York Times* featured the site as a "micropatronage" site for artists.

"Money has always been a huge barrier to creativity," says Perry Chen, cofounder of Kickstarter, in the article. "We all have a lot of ideas we'd like to see get off the ground, but unless you have a rich uncle, you aren't always able to embrace those random ideas."

At the time, the founders handpicked Kickstarter projects, which seemed to come mostly from their social and creative

contacts, though there were plans to eventually open the platform to anyone with a creative idea. Early users and project creators got invitations to Kickstarter, which they could share with others. Kickstarter invitations were also shared over social media and through e-mails between friends, or given to people asking the site directly.

After raising $300,000 from family, friends, and high-profile backers, such as comedian David Cross and Pitchfork Media president Chris Kaskie, Kickstarter was officially launched on April 28, 2009. The platform was initially free to all campaigners, with Kickstarter picking up the processing fees. Charging fees would come later, when the site was open to all, said co-founder Chen.

Projects were curated according to how well they would fit into the "Kickstarter ecosystem," and potential project creators were asked to consider what rewards they would offer participants, how they would spread the word about their project, and what media they would create as part of their campaign. A year later, *Time* magazine named Kickstarter one of the 50 best inventions of 2010, referring to it as "crowdsourced philanthropy."

Initial projects on Kickstarter were small and usually funded—the first successful project was "Drawing for Dollars," which raised $35 from three backers.

From humble beginnings, Kickstarter quickly attracted higher-profile artists, such as Jay Bennett, formerly of Wilco, and pop singer Allison Weiss, who actually gained fame from her promotion on Kickstarter, becoming a poster child for Internet artists.

Other projects proved to be more controversial. Josh Dibb, a.k.a. Deakin of Animal Collective, launched a highly successful Kickstarter project in the site's first year, raising nearly $26,000.

MORE ON KICKSTARTER

LAUNCHED: APRIL 28, 2009

FOUNDED BY: PERRY CHEN, YANCEY STRICKLER, AND CHARLES ADLER

Perry Chen *is also a New York City–based artist who cofounded the Southfirst gallery in Brooklyn in 2001 and has exhibited at the New Museum of Contemporary Art. Kickstarter's focus on artistic and creative projects—Kickstarter asks that all projects create something to share with others—is likely the result of Chen's influence.*

INSPIRED TO INSPIRE

Chen was inspired to create Kickstarter in 2002, when his attempt to bring a band to Jazz Fest in New Orleans failed. He came up with the idea of a website where people could donate funds to causes they supported, and where the project would only be carried out if enough people wanted it to happen.

After his return from New Orleans, Chen met Strickler and Adler in New York City, and the three set to work creating the site that would eventually go live in 2009 as Kickstarter.

The funds were for a trip to perform at the Festival in the Desert in Mali, and the campaign offered donors books, CDs, and a donation to TEMEDT, a Malian organization working to help enslaved Tuareg people. Three years later, donors had yet to receive any of the rewards. Dibb explained to Pitchfork that all funds had been donated to TEMEDT after he became uncomfortable with the idea of asking people to pay for his trip to Africa.

More controversy surrounds celebrities and high-profile artists who use crowdfunding to finance large projects, such as a movie based on the *Veronica Mars* series, which raised $5.7 million, and Zach Braff's film *Wish I Was Here*, which raised over $3.1 million. Users criticized Kickstarter for allowing celebrities and people with presumed large personal worth to use the site, which they perceived as being intended for campaigners who actually need the financial backing. Kickstarter responded by saying high-profile campaigns draw hundreds of new donors who go on to contribute to other projects.

STARTING LINE UP : COMPANIES AHEAD OF THE GAME

1999

Wikipedia launched as free access Internet encyclopedia, where users contribute to articles.

2003

GETAFREELANCER launched in Sweden, later renamed freelancer.com. Image: Matt Barriel, CEO

ELANCE launched to support contractors and third-party services online. Image: Fabio Rosati, CEO

2001

oDesk founded as a service marketplace and work log.

2004

Testy fans that expect quick results on campaigns they fund can also prove to be difficult. *Veronica Mars* creator Rob Thomas, who launched the Kickstarter movie project, eventually passed on the project, saying that it would cost around $2 million just to send the T-shirts, DVDs, and other rewards to donors.

"If we get bad press at the end of the movie because of poor fulfillment, I think it would scare off other studios from doing this," he told the *Wall Street Journal* in 2013.

Fully funded projects that don't deliver also cause major controversy on Kickstarter, and there's usually no way to recover funds once they've been paid out.

Erik Chevalier, who raised over $120,000 to create a board game inspired by long-form, character-driven tabletop gaming, called "The Doom That Came to Atlantic City," ended up walking away with the funds, citing legal issues, technical problems, and moving expenses as complications. As for the funds: No one saw or heard of them again. "Unfortunately I can't give any type of

REDDIT an entertainment, social networking, and news crowd-sourced website founded.

8002

PATREON a crowdsource platform that allows users to become patrons for online artists launched.

2010

2005

GIVEFORWARD a donation based crowdfunding platform for personal causes launched. Image: Desiree Vargas Wrigley and Ethan Austin, cofounders

MICROVENTURES equity crowdfunding website for early stage companies launched.

2013

schedule for the repayment as I left my job to do this project and must find work again," said Chevalier on the campaign page.

While crowdfunding expert Ethan Mollick wrote in his article "The Dynamics of Crowdfunding: An Exploratory Study" that only 3.6 percent of successfully funded projects failed to deliver, plenty of projects made it into that category. Among them are Luci, a device that promised to induce lucid dreaming, which was canceled amid accusations of fraud, but not before raising raising $320,410. There was also Kobe Red, a supposed beef jerky start-up that raised more than $120,000 before it was revealed to be a scam.

Kickstarter has some basic controls in place to prevent campaign scams, including identity verification for campaign creators and project assessment for unique creative contributions; in other words, you can't use the platform to raise money for your vacation fund.

Since the introduction of "Launch Now," Kickstarter's new algorithm-based approval system, which no longer requires human approval for new campaigns, more and more questionable projects have made it into Kickstarter ecosystem.

Take, for example, the potato salad campaign, which raised over $55,000 for creator Zack Brown, who launched the project with a goal of raising $10 to make a potato salad. Or consider the Pashanin brothers' multiple gaming-focused Kickstarter campaigns, none of which has ever delivered a product.

In February 2012, GoFundMe celebrated raising its first $1 million in a single month, which was soon surpassed by its first $5 million in a single month the following November. As of April 2014, GoFundMe averages $1 million raised per day.

Still, no website is without controversy. GoFundMe has been called out for its refusal to support campaigns associated with abortion, saying that such material is not appropriate for its site. In a message to news website *Salon* (www.salon.com), a GoFundMe representative stated that while campaigns were reviewed on a case-by-case basis, a woman's abortion fund, titled "Bailey's Abortion Fund," was removed from the site because its subject matter was something "GoFundMe would rather not be associated with."

After the initial incident, GoFundMe changed its policies, prohibiting any projects associated with abortion, without exception, stating that campaigns associated with "termination of life" would be banned. Critics noted that this is the same language used by anti-abortion activists who believe in fetal personhood. The policy seems to apply only to campaigns that are pro-choice on the issue; anti-abortion projects are allowed to raise funds on the site.

Salon reported that at least three self-identified anti-abortion campaigns have been allowed to run on the site despite the ban on anything abortion related.

On GoFundMe's Facebook page, users responded in outrage. One asked, "Why are you such a misogynistic and racist company?," and others vowed never to spend another dime on the site.

CAUSE IN QUESTION

Divisive political issues—such as as marriage equality, abortion, and police violence—can quickly go viral, making a lot of money for crowd-funding sites in the process. GoFundMe made about $42,000 from the Memories Pizza campaign, which raised funds for a pizza shop that refused to cater a same-sex wedding. Campaigns support-ing Darren Wilson, the police officer who shot teenager Michael Brown in August 2014, raised more than $430,000 on the site.

MORE ON GOFUNDME

DONATION-BASED
CROWDFUNDING PLATFORM

GoFundMe.com *allows people to raise money for life events such as weddings, graduations, illnesses, and accidents. Brad Damphousse and Andrew Ballester—who had earlier collaborated to found Paygr, a site for people to sell their services, billed an "eBay for local commerce"—founded GoFundMe in May 2010. Frustrated by the difficult process of opening a savings account online for his vacation, Damphousse opened a Web-based "social" savings account—one that allowed other users to donate money to his fund. From this early beginning, GoFundMe was born.*

MAKING THE BEST OF IT

Originally launched as "CreateAFund" in 2008, the name changed when upgrades were made to the site in early 2010. The site then took off as a personal crowdfunding platform.

While not exclusively a personal cause platform, the absence of a rewards system lends itself more to donations and causes than creative project funding.

From slow beginnings as a subscription fund-raising service for small charities, the fledgling start-up grew into a platform that emphasizes users' personal stories to fuel support for individual campaigns.

Other controversial campaigns include a fund-raising effort on behalf of Memories Pizza, whose owner told a local Indiana news station that she would not cater a gay wedding. The campaign raised $842,387 on GoFundMe in April of 2015. Campaigns were also created to raise money for Officer Darren Wilson, the police officer who shot and killed Michael Brown in Ferguson, Missouri.

Although GoFundMe has adopted rules banning certain campaigns, it has been criticized for its lax restrictions around accountability, with the *International Business Times* pointing to the site's inability to guarantee the authenticity of campaigns.

SAVING THE DAY
FOR START-UPS

ANGEL INVESTING FACTS

Angel investors are individuals (often retired entrepreneurs or executives) who provide capital in exchange for ownership equity in a business.

AngelList started as an online forum for technology, but has become a website for angel investors, start-up companies, and those who'd like to work for them.

Initial investments from angel investors vary greatly, depending on both the start-up and the investor. Investments can start as small as $20,000 and range up to more than $1 million.

Entrepreneurs Naval Ravikant and Babak Nivi founded AngelList in 2010.

In 2014 500 Startups, a start-up accelerator, used AngelList to launch 500 Women, a syndicate for start-ups with at least one female founder.

Kevin Rose, a general partner at Google Ventures, has funded notable companies such as Square, Twitter, and Foursquare.

Yahoo! CEO Marissa Mayer

Marissa Mayer, CEO of Yahoo!, has contributed to Getaround, Square, and up-and-comer Periscope (periscope.io), which offers actionable business data.

Launch Angels (launch-angels.com) collects money from accredited investors in order to fund start-ups. It's also the first and only woman-led fund, and it invests exclusively in women-owned businesses.

In 2014, Launch Angels made news as the first venture fund providing seed funding for companies with LGBT founders and managers.

The VentureOut Fund will raise $2 million for 10 to 15 start-ups breaking into the venture capital world—a world traditionally filled with straight white men.

PLATFORMS WITH PROMISE

FIND THE RIGHT FUNDING

S ome crowdfunding sites have become major players, like Kickstarter and Indiegogo, while others enjoy serving smaller, more dedicated markets. Here's a look at some other crowdfunding notables.

SELLABAND (SELLABAND.COM) 2006

Sellaband is a music website that helps artists raise funds from fans to record professional albums. Founded by former executives of Sony, Shell, and BMG and headquartered in Amsterdam, Sellaband primarily targets European artists, though American artists are also featured. The site filed for bankruptcy in January 2010, only to relaunch a few days later after an investor stepped forward. There are over 700 registered artists on Sellaband.

PROSPER (PROSPER.COM) 2006

Prosper is the first peer-to-peer lending marketplace in the United States, with more than $2 billion in funded loans and over 2.2 million registered members. Based in San Francisco, Prosper allows borrowers to request personal loans anywhere from $2,000 to $35,000. To be considered for funding, borrowers may submit not only their credit scores, but also personal endorsements, community affiliations, and descriptions of how they intend to use the loan. Prosper uses preset rates determined by the platform evaluating each prospective borrower's credit risk.

LENDING CLUB (LENDINGCLUB.COM) 2006

Lending Club is a San Francisco–based peer-to-peer lender that has financed over $6.2 billion in loans. Lending Club was the first P2P lender to register its offerings as securities with the Securities and Exchange Commission and offers loan trading on a secondary market. In December 2014, the platform raised almost $900 million in the largest technology initial public offering of 2014. The company is now valued at $8.5 billion.

WEPAY (WEPAY.COM) 2008

WePay is an online payment service provider that focuses exclusively on crowdfunding platforms, marketplaces, and small-business software. WePay was inspired by founder Rich Aberman's own troubles getting funds to pay for his brother's bachelor party. After studying PayPal's weaknesses, Aberman asked cofounder Bill Clerico to help him solve his problem, and the two created WePay. WePay offers a flexible user experience while protecting against fraud by using social data connections.

IOBY (IOBY.ORG) 2008

Ioby stands for In Our Back Yards, a "crowd-resourcing" platform for individuals leading neighborhood projects. The mission of Ioby is to strengthen neighborhoods by supporting community leaders who want to make positive changes. According to the site, crowd-resourcing combines crowdfunding with resource organizing. The platform gives individuals the ability to organize monetary capital as well as social capital, in-kind donations, volunteer time, and advocacy. Since its inception, Ioby has raised more than $1 million for 424 successfully funded projects.

ROCKETHUB **(ROCKETHUB.COM) 2010**

RocketHub is a crowdfunding platform launched in 2010 by artists: musician-filmmaker Brian Meece, actor-singer Jed Cohen, musician and linguist Alon Hillel Tuch, and tech writer Vladimir Vukicevic. The platform enables direct-to-fan social media outreach and fund-raising, and it allows for project leaders to keep funds even if the goal isn't met. RocketHub has actively advocated for the JOBS Act, which will open the doors to larger crowdfunding opportunities, by testifying before Congress.

SPACEHIVE **(SPACEHIVE.COM) 2011**

SpaceHive is a crowdfunding platform for civic projects such as playgrounds and parks geared toward design profession- als, locals, and public organizations improving community infrastructure. The six-person London-based team has already funded over £1 million in projects in the United Kingdom. The site allows cash raised to be combined with grants and other revenue streams.

CATARSE **(CATARSE.ME/EN) 2011**

Catarse is a crowdfunding website headquartered in Brazil and inspired by Kickstarter. The idea behind Catarse is to democ- ratize fund-raising so that any Brazilian with a creative project can get the funds he or she needs to complete original projects. The company works as a unit with no official CEO or director, and it uses a collective process to make decisions. Catarse is less product-based than Kickstarter, and many of its projects have cultural or social goals instead of material-oriented ones.

MICROVENTURES **(MICROVENTURES.COM) 2011**

MicroVentures is an equity crowdfunding website that offers donors the opportunity to invest in early-stage companies. Currently available only to accredited investors, this platform allows start-ups, businesses, and services to raise funds from venture capitalists and investors. MicroVentures raised $20 million in its first two years of operation, spread among 45 companies that include Twitter, Facebook, and Yelp.

NEIGHBORLY **(NEIGHBORLY.COM/GO) 2015**

Neighborly promises to connect users with opportunities to earn income by investing in civic projects. Its mission is to demystify and democratize access to the municipal securities market, making it easy for midcareer professionals to invest disposable income in their own community. Named one of TechCrunch's four favorite companies from the 500 Start-ups Demo Day in October 2014, Neighborly was scheduled to launch in summer 2015.

CITIZINVESTOR **(CITIZINVESTOR.COM) 2012**

Citizinvestor is a civic engagement platform for local government projects, empowering citizens to invest in the local community. Government entities or their official partners are invited to start project campaigns on the site, and citizens are invited to donate tax-deductible funds to projects of their choice. Projects are not developed unless they reach 100 percent of the stated goal, and the model runs on a donation-based platform, where no rewards are given for pledges.

IT'S ALL ABOUT YOUCARING

The goal of YouCaring is to give people the opportunity to help their neighbors, friends, and family meet both their financial and emotional needs. YouCaring offers completely free online fund-raising—that means no credit card service charges, collection fees, or up-front costs to start a campaign. It runs a platform that relies on the generosity of the YouCaring community in the form of donations to keep the site running—and that's it. Like many other donation-based crowdfunding sites, it caters to campaigns that pay medical bills, adoption fees, and tuition. About 35 percent of campaigners are 50 or older.

In 2014, the largest crowdfunding-review site, CrowdsUnite (crowdsunite.com), named YouCaring the top overall platform based on its ease of use, customer support, and funding.

Despite not paying for any marketing or PR, YouCaring has become the Web's second most popular site dedicated exclusively to fund-raising for philanthropic needs.

"It's always been our mission to provide the best platform for people in need," said YouCaring founder and CEO Brock Ketcher. "We hope this recognition ultimately benefits our fund-raisers and their worthy causes."

CAMPAIGNS YOU CAN COPY

HOW TO GO ABOVE AND BEYOND

DEVELOP A COMPLETE IDEA

One of the biggest mistakes Kickstarter creators make is launching a campaign without having a fleshed-out idea. You shouldn't launch campaigns to create a board game if you have no idea what kind of work that entails, just like you can't build a digital watch if you don't know the first thing about electronic hardware.

Ryan Grepper, creator of the Coolest Cooler, had been working as a self-described inventor for years before developing the product that finally took off. "Nine or 10 years ago, I was making a blender out of a weed wacker, putting an old car stereo into a cooler," said Grepper. He asked friends and family for advice on all his projects, and he got better at tuning into what people might want and what projects might be worth trying to get funded online.

Feedback from friends, family, and neighbors is also an invaluable way to refine your project proposal and make sure it answers users' initial questions. Reaching out to your personal network helps build a base of initial backers for launch. So is

DO

Follow your passion

Develop your ideas

Appeal to your friends, family, and community

Be patient and follow through

DON'T

Be swayed: trust your vision

Attempt to fundraise before fully developing your idea

Run a campaign with zero support from your social circle

Give up

reviewing already-existing projects or ideas so you have a good idea of how you size up to the competition, and make sure you have legal advice in case you run into any trouble.

The insanely popular "Exploding Kittens" card game, which raised over $8 million on Kickstarter, was originally called "Bomb Squad" until it was suggested that the creators change the name "because…the Internet," said cocreator Elan Lee.

BUILD ON YOUR IDEAS

Offer something people really want, and then continue building with that idea, making a better version of it each time.

The most successful Kickstarter campaign, Pebble Watch, was developed after creator Eric Migicovsky got plenty of customer feedback from his earlier project, a watch called InPulse. "We talked to these customers, got their detailed feedback, learned what was missing, what features they wish they had," Migicovsky

[
81,000 projects have been successfully funded on Kickstarter.
]

told Xprize (xprize.org), an educational nonprofit, about the development of Pebble Watch.

"Before we ever launched on Kickstarter, we had feedback from 1,500 real customers," he said. "So when we designed the Pebble Watch, we made exactly what the public wanted."

Grepper, the creator behind the second most popular Kickstarter campaign, "The Coolest Cooler," also went through an earlier version of his product before designing the model that would ultimately prove successful. This first version of the Coolest Cooler hit Kickstarter back in 2013, and fell more than $20,000 short of its goal.

"As most people who are first launching a project on Kickstarter do, you do some research, you put the product out there, and you hope for and secretly expect that because this idea is great, magically it will get funded," Grepper told Mashable, an online media website, about his first campaign. "It was very disappointing."

The campaign made many mistakes that first-time campaigners make: setting the target funding goal too high, launching with an unfinished design, and not waiting for the right moment. Grepper initially introduced the Coolest Cooler in the winter, when users weren't looking to buy summer gear.

SET AN APPROPRIATE GOAL

The Coolest Cooler failed the first time around even though it raised $100,000. Why? Because Grepper had set his goal for $125,000. One of the most important steps in making sure you have a successful campaign is ensuring you have an appropriate funding goal.

The first thing you need to assess is what stage of the project you're raising funds for. Do you need enough to complete the entire project, or are you simply trying to raise enough money to take your project to the next level? Think about your entire project as you envision it, and figure out if there are milestones along the way that you need to get to before you can finish. Is there equipment you need to buy, space you need to rent, or contractors you need to hire?

Develop a complete plan for your campaign, including a finished design and budget. Sharing your complete design, and even more ideally, a finished prototype of your work, will ensure that users trust your ability to complete the project.

Make sure your fund-raising goal allows you to complete important milestones but is not so high that you'll be unlikely to raise the money. Offering users the chance to help you on your first steps is important, even if you're unable to promise a finished product as a reward.

Also remember to include the cost of shipping and handling in your rewards costs. It's easy to forget to include postage stamps, transportation costs, T-shirt printing, and designer costs into your budget, but all these miscellaneous expenses add up.

DESIGN, AND DESIGN AGAIN

Be fully prepared before your launch date. Make sure you have all the media you need (video, press release, and prototype) before liftoff.

"There's a ton of design that went into this campaign," said Exploding Kittens cocreator Lee. "I think the version of the video on the Kickstarter page is version 14, and months went into designing and redesigning the wording, the art, and the game."

Timing can also be a big factor in launching your campaign, as Grepper found out with the Coolest Cooler. He initially launched his campaign in winter. "We thought tailgating folks would want it and Christmas would work," Grepper told CNBC. "But I hadn't done enough homework." He relaunched his Kickstarter in the summer, which proved to be a key factor in his success the second time around. "The cooler market is hot in the summer," Grepper said. "That was one of those hindsight realizations."

Building up a support group of backers before debuting your campaign is equally important. "Using the folks from last time around and other fans, we made a bigger splash that had a ripple effect," Grepper said. "The campaign starts when it goes up online, but the biggest variables are the work that goes into the campaign, connecting with your backers before you go live."

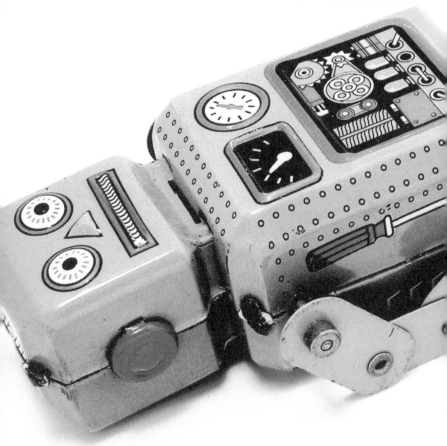

CAMPAIGNS THAT COULDN'T CUT IT

LARGE GOALS, LITTLE
FOLLOW-THROUGH

While crowdfunding has helped support innovative projects and game changers across many different fields, not all campaigns have experienced success. There are a number of campaigns that have not reached their goals, but more unsettling are campaigns that reached their funding goal without producing results.

Here are some crowdfunding failures, plus tips on how not to follow in their footsteps.

SMARTY RING

Smarty Ring is just one in a series of wearable technologies aimed at taking the next step beyond watches and one of a number of questionable campaigns.

Smarty Ring is a particularly well-funded campaign of this type—its first iteration yielded almost $300,000 from over 1,500 funders. Promising to let you control your smartphone from the small ring interface, the campaign page says you can "be part of the tech revolution" by getting "instant alerts on your finger." The campaign was so successful that Smarty Ring started a second campaign before the first one was over; this second campaign collected another $102,000 from 716 users.

The pages for both campaigns are riddled with user comments about the lack of updates and accusations of scamming. "Once again another month has passed and another month of no refunds. Your updates are meaningless. Your words are empty. You show no tangible updates, just empty words," says one user on the campaign site, which can be seen at Indiegogo.

Many funders have filed a case with the Internet and Computing Core Certification program, which is cosponsored by

DID YOU KNOW

Sam Hyde, creator of Million Dollar Extreme, a troll, prank, and comedy group, once created an Indiegogo campaign called "Kickstarter TV: Where Idiots Go to Spend Money on Crap." The campaign was used to honor the rewards from a previous prank campaign and fund Kickstarter TV.

the FBI and the National White Collar Crime Center.

Other users just request updates on the project, though it has been months since any were posted to the campaign pages. "Do you think the Smarty Ring creator even visits the comment section any longer? If so, it would be nice if they post a few pictures of their progress," said another donor on the campaign.

According to tech site Gizmodo, a functional smart ring is incredibly hard to make due to the difficulty in fitting all the necessary components into a small device—a feat that would tricky to accomplish even with a larger device. Jawbone, a well-known manufacturer of wearable activity trackers, had to be taken off the market for a year after an initially awful first run due to technical issues—and its product is a much larger bracelet.

Finding room for all the sensors, as well as a battery that will power the device, has proved difficult on wearable technology, as the miniaturization of technology hasn't yet reached that scale.

PID-CONTROLLED ESPRESSO MACHINE

The Kickstarter page promised to create a home espresso machine providing commercial-quality coffee at a low price, but the concept was actually too good to be true.

The PID-Controlled Espresso Machine campaign page is impressive, listing a whole range of technical specs, including which kind of espresso shots the machine would be able to produce, the capacity of the tank, and even what color models would be available.

The group of young engineers, who call themselves ZPM, collected over $365,000 from 1,546 backers, but the group has not delivered on a single promise in three years. Sporadic updates to the campaign page informed donors of software-development issues, hardware problems, and burned coffee.

Over 1,000 user comments express dissatisfaction with the group's process, calling the members "thieves" and asking for transparency. "I have no doubt that the initial state of the project was misguided optimism and hubris," said one donor in the comments page. "But to wait this long for a description of what has happened, how funds were spent, what's left, and how we move forward is not very reasonable."

An article on technology news and review site SlashGear announced in January 2015—a full three years after the project's initial funding—that the chief operations officer of ZPM left the group in December 2014 and took most of the team with her. The remaining team members report that without the COO and no additional funding, they have no way of moving forward on the project. "While we've looked into several other financing options, after serious consideration, we reached the decision to shut the company down. We are currently ending all operations," said one member of the team on networking site Reddit (reddit.com). "We're having conversations with several other parties to see if we can't create a situation where your pledges are still honored and you guys get something for all your support of this project," the team member continued. The Kickstarter campaign page, however, has yet to be updated.

TRIGGERTRAP

Triggertrap creates hardware and software products that work with SLR cameras. The company started in July 2011, when Haje Jan Kamps started a Kickstarter campaign to raise funds for the creation of a new type of camera trigger. The initial funding goal of $25,000 was exceeded by more than $50,000, and the project, which had almost 900 supporters, delivered three times as many camera triggers as originally expected.

In 2013 Triggertrap Ada was successfully crowdfunded, again via Kickstarter, and promised donors a camera trigger that functioned through mobile devices. The project encountered many difficulties, including software-development setbacks that hindered project goals, and delays that put the team a year behind schedule.

In an article posted to blog-publishing platform Medium, Triggertrap chief Kamps discussed exactly where his team went wrong. First, they completely blew their budget. "One of the first things you do when you're planning to bring a new product to market is to create a project budget," wrote Kamps. "So that's what we did."

From its prior experience making other trigger devices and funding them through crowdsourcing campaigns, the company estimated its comprehensive budget, including the cost of promoting it on Kickstarter. The team came in 2 percent

HAJE JAN KAMPS

Triggertrap CEO Haje Jan Kamps is a bit of a Danish Renaissance man, as an inventor, author, freelance writer, journalist, photographer, and editor. Currently living in London, Kamps is best known for running the hugely popular photography blog Photocritic. He's also written and contributed to more than 10 books on photography.

under budget for campaign promotion—the only part of the project that stayed on track.

On the same day as the campaign launch, the team received notice from a major camera manufacturer that took issue with the name the company had chosen for the device. Triggertrap's legal budget was then allocated toward the registration of new logos and trademarks in an attempt to avoid a lawsuit.

The next setback came when it was notified that the microprocessor it originally wanted to use for the device didn't have enough memory. Much more than the originally budgeted amount was spent redesigning the product and finishing a slew of prototypes. By the time that process was complete, the company had spent five times what was originally budgeted.

That wasn't the end of its troubles. After the redesign, the cost to make the product rose significantly, and the company realized that to make the newly designed product, it would have to sell the model for three times the originally estimated price point. "The problem we're now facing is the deal breaker: At the price point we're now looking at ($350 instead of $99), the product doesn't make as much sense anymore," wrote Kamps.

Preorder sales confirmed that fact. Though 4,000 people on the company's mailing list had expressed interest in placing an order, only 1.5 percent actually placed one after learning of the new $350 price.

And so, in a series of unfortunate fell swoops, the project was scrapped. Kamps and Triggertrap were gracious enough not only to write about the experience and why the project failed, but also to give six tips:

I. **Fail faster.** "There were quite a few points throughout the Triggertrap Ada project where we should have taken stock and pulled the plug earlier, or at least taken action when we realized things were moving in the wrong direction," wrote Kamps.

II. **Don't let money mask the problem.** The incredible success of the Kickstarter campaign, and the large amounts of money in the bank, made the creators lose sight of some of the problems, which was a big mistake.

III. **Employ tight project management.** Manage your resources well, and make sure you know how much you're spending on the project materials and development.

IV. **Get the right skills.** Make sure you or your team are well equipped to handle the problems you may encounter in trying to deliver a product.

V. **Avoid uncontrollable change or continuous growth (scope creep).** "This is the one I really punish myself for every day, not least because it's such an obvious mistake," wrote Kamps. Think through the implications of design changes and the cost of substituting materials, especially after you've already created a budget.

VI. **Don't be naive.** Make sure you know everything you can about how to carry out the project before launching a campaign. "A healthy dose of realism and skepticism—and taking professional advice earlier—would have gone a long way," Kamps wrote.

JONATHAN YAFFE

ANYROAD CEO
GIVES LEGS TO
MICROENTREPRENEURS

AnyRoad enables microentrepreneur tour guides to run their businesses online and compete on a global scale. The company, started by brothers Jonathan and Daniel Yaffe, empowers travelers to discover, vet, and book tour guides' on demand in 104 countries. Yaffe took a moment to speak with our team about AnyRoad and crowdsourcing.

Why did you start your business?

We started AnyRoad because we saw a huge infrastructural gap in the tourism industry. We realized that some of the most incredible experiences, awe-inspiring tours, and guides have never been online. If we can book hotels, taxis, and flights from our phones, why aren't we able to find an incredible guide and book her instantly?

What drew you to tourism?

The tourism industry globally employs 1 in 8 people; by giving this industry the tools to modernize, we're able to democratize the flow of tourism dollars, and level the playing field while connecting travelers to the best tours around. Our vision is that a Chinese family traveling to the middle of the Amazon rainforest can find, vet, and pay for an incredible Chinese-speaking guide—from their phone on the way to the airport. We're working to connect modern-day explorers with the best experiences that exist, most of which cannot currently be found online.

What do you see as the future of crowdsourcing?

A decade ago, people often traveled with one guidebook, and followed the advice of a single writer, creating "backpacker routes" and steering travelers to the same worn hostels, the same crowded restaurants, and the same sites. The idea that any one person or website knows the best things to do globally is an antiquated myth perpetuated by the Lonely Planets and Rick Steves of the world. Now, with the emergence and domination of crowdsourced recommendations and inventory, a door is opened to true discovery with help from locals, other travelers, and the professional guides who know their communities the best.

So you are completely disrupting the tourism industry?

We chose to start with professional tour guides, because it is a $16 billion industry that is 97 percent offline and still dominated by cash, international bank transfers, and phone calls. Largely due to this lack of access, large corporations, like Greyline and Abercrombie and Kent, have a huge advantage when competing for tourists. By simply bringing these guides online and making them visible, AnyRoad is able to measurably shift the flow of money into many heavily touristed areas, benefiting the communities themselves and their development.

MUCH MORE THAN MONEY

AIRBNB TURNS YOUR SPACE INTO A MARKETPLACE

Airbnb users have a plethora of choices. Property listings range from shared rooms in the suburbs to beautiful high-rise apartments with city views. Then there's everything in between: tree houses, boats, yurts—you name it.

Airbnb provides the digital infrastructure to make rentals possible, providing individuals with listings and space to promote and market their space with useful information, such as prices, amenities, photos, and guest reviews.

Airbnb founders Brian Chesky and Joe Gebbia created the initial concept for AirBed & Breakfast during the Industrial Design Conference in 2007. The first iteration of the site was made in conjunction with the conference, offering attendees short-term living quarters, breakfast, and business networking opportunities for individuals who were unable to book a hotel.

Chesky and Gebbia were roommates at the time, having just moved to San Francisco in October 2007, and they could not afford the rent on their loft in the city. They decided to make ther living room into a bed-and-breakfast.

Nathan Blecharczyk, Joe Gebbia, and Brian Chesky (cofounders of Airbnb) lie for a portrait on an air bed in their headquarters in San Francisco, California.

In 2008 Nathan Blecharczyk joined the team as a third cofounder. He helped Chesky and Gebbia focus on high-profile events hosted in San Francisco.

Capitalizing on the 2008 Democratic National Convention in Denver, the founders found hosts in the area to offer room rentals. Then they used the Democratic primary in promotional materials for the site. Initial funding for the project was procured by selling cereals inspired by presidential candidates Barack Obama and John McCain—the group raised $30,000 from the sale of 800 boxes of "Obama O's" and "Cap'n McCains." The success of their fund-raising campaign caught the attention of Paul Graham of the Y Combinator, an incubator that provides funding for new start-ups.

"If you can convince people to pay $40 for a box of cereal, you can probably convince them to pay to sleep on each other's air mattresses," Graham told the founders. "You guys are in."

In January 2009, Y Combinator invited Chesky, Gebbia, and Blecharczyk to the incubator's winter session, where they gained $20,000 to put toward travel necessary to promote the site. By the time they returned to San Francisco, they had a profitable business model and a fully built website.

In March 2009, the website was shortened to Airbnb.com, and the business offerings were expanded to include shared spaces, entire homes, apartments, and all manner of sleeping arrangements, like tree houses, tipis, and private islands. A year later the founders found themselves with 15 employees, $7.2 million raised from venture capital firms, and over 700,000 bookings through the site. The rest is history.

Much of the site's success has been attributed to the ingenuity and persistence of the founders, exemplified by the cereal boxes they promoted on the Internet to gain the capital they needed to move the project forward.

Fred Wilson, a partner at the New York venture firm Union Square Ventures, which initially passed on the project, now displays a box of Obama O's in his office as a reminder. "We made the classic mistake that all investors make," Wilson wrote on his blog, AVC.com. "We focused too much on what they were doing at the time and not enough on what they could do, would do, and did do."

Although Airbnb has been recognized as a leading innovator on the Web, named the Breakout App at the 2011 South by Southwest conference, and listed in the *New York Times* as one of the next generation of multibillion-dollar start-ups, the site is not without its fair share of controversy.

In both San Francisco and New York, the platform has raised a host of issues regarding regulation and social impact. Rentals of less than 30 days are illegal in most multiunit buildings in both cities, and are often prohibited by lease agreements. Additionally, policymakers and activists fear that scarce rental housing is being diverted into Airbnb markets to the detriment of thousands of city residents who can no longer find affordable housing.

"Behind buzzwords like 'the sharing economy' and 'disruptive,' Airbnb as a platform simply allows many of their hosts to operate unlicensed, unregulated and untaxed hotels in residential neighborhoods," states Inside Airbnb, an activist website that compiles data from Airbnb listings to show the impact on local communities.

Murray Cox, the activist behind the site, argues that Airbnb misinforms the public, giving incorrect information about the true nature of the listings on the platform. "Looking at the calendars and reviews for the entire homes and apartments, I found that more than 90 percent of them were available for more than 60 days out of the year, and on average received a review

DID YOU KNOW

There were 16,483 private rentals listed on Airbnb as of late 2014. There were only 2,652 in 2010. The company initially started with just one listing: the founders' own apartment. Some of the growth is attributed to the economic crash of 2008, when many people were looking to save money and empower themselves. People liked that they were paying a person, not a corporation.

from a guest once a month," said Cox in an interview with progressive online news source AlterNet. "This directly refuted Airbnb's claims that 87 percent of Airbnb hosts share the home in which they live.'"

Airbnb has also drawn criticism from policymakers like New York State Senator Liz Krueger, who represents Manhattan's Upper East Side. "Airbnb doesn't seem to have very much respect for the law," she said in an interview with the *San Francisco Chronicle*. "I understand that they view themselves as a new model of economic activity, dynamism, and change. But their assumption that regulations to protect the interests of the entire community shouldn't [apply to] the online model is unacceptable to me."

Many policymakers and Airbnb advocates argue that the difficulties faced by the platform are the result of its new and innovative nature as well as the inherent difficulty in addressing these concerns with old regulations. "Old regulatory frameworks never contemplated these new disruptive businesses," said Jeff Jordan, a partner at venture capital firm Andreessen Horowitz. "There is often friction and learning as that happens. Airbnb is working hard with municipalities to be a responsible company."

Innovation and creative approaches to problem-solving have their limits, and Airbnb is a perfect example of a crowdsourcing darling that faces its own slew of problems as it matures into a more stable company.

Only time will tell if bringing crowdsourcing off the Web and into the home will prove to be an enduring phenomenon or just the latest Internet trend.

GETTING THERE TOGETHER
HOPSTOP FACTS

1 **HopStop** is an online transit guide offering crowdsourced subway, bus direction, and maps for over 140 cities worldwide.

2 **HopStop was founded** in 2005 and named one of the top 100 fastest-growing software companies in 2011.

3 **Inspired by the success** of Waze, the GPS navigation app that also lets users submit alerts for accidents and traffic jams, HopStop Live lets users report underground delays and alternate bus routes.

4 **HopStop** was purchased by Apple in 2013.

5 **The app covers** 700 transit agencies in 140 cities worldwide and features 20,000 lines and 750,000 stops.

6 **HopStop** has over 2 million monthly active users.

UBER ENTERS THE ECONOMY

THE END OF CABS?

Uber is a crowdsourcing company headquartered in San Francisco that develops, markets, and operates a mobile phone app–based transportation network. It is now available in 55 countries and more than 250 cities worldwide. Uber allows users to submit a trip request, which is then routed to crowdsourced taxi drivers, who accept trip requests and make a commission from each ride.

The idea for Uber came to cofounder Travis Kalanick in 2008, when he was at a conference in Paris and could not find a cab. His friend and StumbleUpon cofounder Garrett Camp told him of an idea for a luxury car service that didn't cost $700 per ride. The service launched as UberCab two years later in San Francisco and was available as a mobile app for both iPhones and Androids.

The crowdsourced transportation idea quickly took off and has been highly successful in procuring funding for the company. Uber received venture funding in late 2010 from angel investors in Silicon Valley, and in early 2011, it raised more than $11.5 million from funding led by Benchmark Capital. Later that same year, several investors, including Goldman Sachs, Menlo Ventures, and Bezos Expeditions added $32 million to the pot, bringing Uber's total funding to $49.5 million.

In December 2014, the *Wall Street Journal* reported that Uber had raised a total of $1.2 billion from investors, and the company is now valued at $41 billion.

Since its inception, Uber has serviced an average of 1 million rides in more than 250 cities daily.

Over time, the initial idea of basing the service on luxury limousine services has changed into an on-demand cab alternative, which is accessible through mobile phones.

Since its inception, Uber has grown into a behemoth of transportation, providing an average of one million rides in more than 250 cities daily. The network adds 50,000 new drivers monthly and paid out $650 million to its US drivers in the last quarter of 2014 alone.

Drivers in crowdsourced transportation networks report enjoying flexible hours, better pay, and a better work-life balance because of the availability of contract work on sites like Uber, and 71 percent of drivers report their income is better since signing up.

Despite being a venture capital darling and providing additional income and jobs for many individuals, Uber has encountered much opposition. The app faces opposition from taxi companies that have taken a hit to their business from projects like Uber, Sidecar, and Lyft. A report from the San Francisco Municipal Transportation Agency, released in 2014, confirmed that in the prior 15 months, traditional cab services in the city had fallen by 65 percent.

While some cab drivers protest the incursion on their market by apps like Uber, others have taken to purchasing a license that allows them to work for Uber as well as their traditional employers.

Uber has also faced protests from its own drivers, who bemoan the company's stance on tips: Uber does not yet allow operators to collect tips on rides in their network. "Uber tells the customer that their tip for the driver is included, but it isn't," said one Uber SUV driver, Hilal Aissani, in an article from *Business Insider*. "Drivers never see a dollar of that tip money."

Competition is also high in crowdsourced transportation, especially from Uber's main rival, Lyft, a transportation network company also based in San Francisco. It runs a similar peer-to-peer ridesharing network, where passengers in need of a ride can connect with drivers through the platform. Lyft operates in 65 cities in the United States, and it has raised $333.5 million from venture capital firms.

Logan Green and John Zimmer launched Lyft in 2012; they had previously operated a network called Zimride, which focused on ridesharing for longer city-to-city trips. Lyft originally operated on a donation-based platform, where passengers gave a donation to drivers after receiving their services. In 2013, Lyft changed its policies, charging passengers per ride based on the distance and duration of the ride.

Lyft has been compared to Uber, and it has been called the "community-driven" platform that encourages friendship between drivers and passengers. Uber, meanwhile, is perceived as pushing more of a top-down hierarchy.

In 2013 San Francisco Mayor Ed Lee proclaimed July 13 as Lyft Day, and well-known venture capital investor Scott Weiss said that Andreessen Horowitz invested in Lyft because of its strong sense of community and transparency. "Lyft is a real community—with both the drivers and riders being inherently social—making real friendships and saving money," Weiss wrote on his blog.

The rivalry spawned a pricing war between the two in January 2014, when both Uber and Lyft slashed their rates to below taxi-rate level in many US cities, affecting the income of many of the drivers on both networks.

"We aren't getting the full pay we used to," said Luke McCready, who began driving for Lyft after quitting his Wells Fargo sales job, in an article in *Fortune* magazine.

While Uber slashed its prices by 20 percent, it also increased the commission it takes from every ride, from 5 percent to 20 percent. Lyft, meanwhile, slashed its prices an average of 30 percent across its network, but it took a different approach with its drivers, eliminating its 20 percent commission to support its

community during the price-drop wars. In June 2014, *Forbes* declared Uber the winner of the rivalry, citing Uber's $17 billion valuation, compared with Lyft's less than $1 billion.

Uber and Lyft are not alone in the ridesharing business; they now share the market with several smaller companies that offer similar services in many major cities.

Sidecar, a transportation network also founded and headquartered in San Francisco, offers ridesharing in 10 cities across the United States. Since it was founded in 2012, the network has facilitated over 10,000 rides and raised over $20 million in seed funding. In fall 2012, shortly after Sidecar launched, the California Public Utilities Commission (CPUC) issued a cease-and-desist letters to Sidecar, Lyft, and Uber, fining each $20,000 for engaging in transportation services without legal right.

The ensuing legislative battles finally ended in 2013, when the CPUC officially recognized companies like Lyft, Sidecar, and Uber as "New Online Enabled Transportation Services" or "Transportation Networked Companies (TNCs)." The new legislation requires that all TNCs run criminal background checks on drivers, establish a driver training program, and procure insurance coverage at a minimum of $1 million per incident.

The newly regulated market continues to encourage the growth of peer-to-peer transit networks, including Wingz (wingz. me) and FlightCar (flightcar.com), which both offer rides to and from the airport, and Hella Rides (hellarides.com), which offers a rideshare network available by invite only, to promote a closer community among drivers and passengers.

KICKSTARTER
KICKS SQUATTERS

WHAT HAPPENED WHEN
AN AIRBNB RENTAL WENT WRONG?

Brothers Maksym and Denys Pashanin have been declared the modern-day Frank and Jesse James of the sharing economy. They stand accused of scamming users on Kickstarter and squatting in a private property via Airbnb.

After paying for a 44-day stay in a private condo in Palm Springs through Airbnb, the Pashanin's decided to stay without further payment. Their decision drew national attention. Kickstarter immediately cancelled Maksym and Denys's campaign for Knuckle Club, a game being developed by their company, Kilobite Inc. Another Pashanin campaign, Confederate Express, has already been fully funded, although donors have little hope of seeing the finished product, much less a refund of their donations.

COMMUNES, CO-OPS, AND SHARED ECONOMIES

LET'S TALK COLLABORATIVE CONSUMPTION

Collaborative consumption is the shared use of a good or service by a group. Instead of one individual incurring the cost of purchasing a good or using a service, the price is divided among a larger group.

Collaboration is leading Internet innovation because it drives down the prices of goods and services, making them more accessible to individuals. Platforms like Airbnb, Uber, and Lyft also provide opportunities for income from already-owned goods.

RENTING

There are many platforms available to rent goods you'd like to try for a fraction of the cost at which you would have to buy them. Getable (getable.com), a start-up founded in 2009 as "Rentcycle," started with a mission to bring the rental industry

Andy Ruben, founder and CEO of Yerdle

online, offering users free reservations and cloud-based business management and product listing support for local rental shops.

Many have compared Getable to OpenTable, the online restaurant reservation site. They share some of the same venture capitalist funders. The newly christened Getable offers in-store rental management for small businesses and is available through the Web and iPad applications.

The app has been shared with 10 early partners in the San Francisco Bay Area, and its developers hope to offer consumers an alternative way of gaining access to something rather than owning it. The new name is meant to give users the sense that any product is accesssible and available on-demand at trusted rental establishments.

Getable recently surpassed 100,000 rental listings, and it has created partnerships with similar renting services like Rent the Runway (renttherunway.com) and Adorn (adorn.com), both of which offer designer goods. The start-up has processed $250,000 in rental transactions so far and has plans to roll out in other cities soon.

Similar to Getable but with a little time on the market, Getaround (getaround.com) is an online car-sharing peer-to-peer service that helps drivers rent cards from private car owners, usually for an hourly rate. Owners set the rental prices on their vehicles and earn a 60 percent commission from the rental revenue.

Getaround launched in May 2011 and is headquartered in San Francisco. Since its inception, the site has received $40 million in seed funding and operates in several US cities, including Austin, Chicago, San Francisco, and San Diego.

The company developed hardware called Getaround Connect, which enables keyless entry to vehicles on its platform through the mobile app. Thanks to this innovation, car owners in the network do not have to be present to accept rental requests, and the availability of vehicles on the platform has increased.

Getaround currently has around 600 cars available through on-demand rental in San Francisco alone.

EXCHANGE

Yerdle (yerdle.com) represents a slightly different take on the sharing model, allowing users to exchange used goods for credits that can be used to buy other on the network. The platform is mobile-based, not neigborhood-based, and it works on a pay-it-forward model. Yerdle encourages users to send goods by mail to other individuals on the network.

Its mission is to make it easier for individuals to share items that are not being used in exchange for items they need, making consumption of new items less necessary. "We dream of a world where it's easier to get a blender that's sitting unused than to buy a new one and pay full price," the company says in its mission statement.

Venmo (venmo.com) is another mobile app that facilitates payments between users, by linking personal bank accounts to profiles on the network. Paying back a friend, neighbor, or housemate is simple and fast—users simply send each other bills for split restaurant checks or money for a round of beers.

Venmo is the brainchild of cofounders Iqram Magdon-Ismail and Andrew Kortina, who came up with the idea for a mobile money service after realizing how inconvenient it was to try paying each other back if they didn't have cash on hand.

"One of the times that we got together, Iqram didn't have his wallet and he ended up writing me a check," recalled Kortina in an interview with *Forbes*. "We thought, 'This is weird that we're still doing this [because] we do everything with our phones.'"

Venmo also features a newsfeed that shares user-generated descriptions of transactions; many are playful or feature emoji, but it never shares the transaction amount.

Venmo does not charge users any fees to receive money from debit cards or for making payments or bank transfers. Venmo makes money when merchants use the network to accept payments, charging them 25¢ per transaction.

SERVICES

Mobile apps and Web platforms that let users market and share their services are on the rise, helping users make some extra cash by sharing their knowledge.

Skillshare (skillshare.com) is a Web platform that allows users to enroll in classes taught by creators around the world. Unlike traditional classroom settings, online classes at Skillshare are taught by industry experts and focus on learning by doing. Courses on the Skillshare network are unaccredited, and anyone who wants to learn can join.

Skillshare launched its first course offerings in August 2012, after raising a total of $10 million in seed funding. It offered students 15 self-paced online courses, in which students collaborated with each other to complete a project. A year later, the platform had more than 250 courses and launched its School of Design as well as the School of MakeOurMark in collaboration with Levi's.

In March 2014, Skillshare moved to a membership model, offering hundreds of courses in design, business, and technology for a $9.95 monthly subscription. It also introduced a new open platform, where any user can teach a course.

YOU CAN DO IT

Creating your own shared economy can be easy. You don't necessarily have to build a complicated Internet infrastructure to assign tasks or share. Think about the common costs, needs, or resources you and a group of friends or family members have in common. From groceries to gardening tools, creative collaborative consumption can save you time and money.

TaskRabbit (taskrabbit.com) is marketplace that allows users to outsource small jobs. Founded in 2008 by Leah Busque when she had no time to buy dog food, the project has received $37.5 million in funding and has over 1.25 million users on its network.

While some users have managed to make TaskRabbit their full-time job, some have critiqued the site for taking a high-percentage commission from each job (60 percent rather than the 15 percent reported on the site).

There are many developments in the field of cooperative skills-sharing and collaborative economics, and this burgeoning field is sure to feature many more platforms in the future. Keep an eye out for new ways to apply the crowdsharing and crowdfunding model to the real world, as innovation knows no bounds.

THEN AND NOW
HOW QUICKLY HAS CROWDFUNDING'S POPULARITY GROWN?

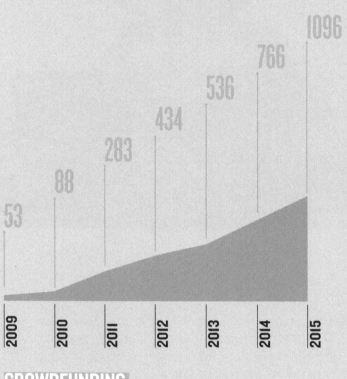

53 — 2009
88 — 2010
283 — 2011
434 — 2012
536 — 2013
766 — 2014
1096 — 2015

CROWDFUNDING PORTALS PER YEAR

HOW TO BUILD BIG

EVERYTHING YOU NEED TO KNOW TO LAUNCH YOUR NEXT PROJECT

There is a great amount of funding to be raised online, but to make the most out of your campaign, care must be taken in how you present your project. Spend as much time as you need to develop your idea. Be clear about how you will achieve your goal; it will make your prospective founders feel much more inclined to give you the funds. Below is a guide on how to prepare for your crowdfunding project.

CHOOSE THE RIGHT PLATFORM

There are as many crowdfunding sites as there are project ideas these days, and picking the right website can make a big difference for your success. It all depends on the type of project you're launching and what your funding goal is.

Personal fund-raising projects, such as paying for medical bills, paying off credit card debt, or funding for a needed surgery, are better suited for sites that cater specifically to the emotional core behind fund-raising. Take a look at sites like YouCaring or GoFundMe for great platforms that will support your cause, charge you little to nothing in fees, and don't require you to meet your funding goal.

Creative and innovative projects, such as producing a new tech toy or creating a new board game, belong on sites like Kickstarter and Indiegogo, which have a wide audience and a lot of fund-raising support. There are a few differences to be aware of—Indiegogo offers a flexible funding model where you can keep funds even if you do not meet your goal, while Kickstarter does not.

Artistic projects, such as fund-raising for a music album, podcast, or concert, can go on artist-specific sites, such as ArtistShare and SellaBand, or traditional funding sites, such as Kickstarter and Indiegogo. There are also monthly crowdfunding models, where fans can become patrons—check out Patreon (patreon.com).

DEFINE YOUR IDEA

Create a business plan with a well-thought-out strategy for how to carry out the idea you have, all the way to distribution. Make sure you are prepared to carry out that plan, and have all the

information you need, including contractor rates, building sche-
mata, material costs, and outsourcing support. This might be a
good time to look into a project manager if you've never handled
a large project and you're dreaming big.

Developing a thorough business plan is the best way to
develop a clear strategy that will help you move forward with
the confidence to share what you have in mind. This will help
later with the presentation of your campaign; the more fully
developed the plan, the more trustworthy you appear to potential investors.

GET FEEDBACK

Remember that business plan you developed in the last step?
Share that plan with friends, family, loved ones, and neighbors.
Ask them to scrutinize your plan and give you completely
honest feedback. This is the time when you can go back and fix
any foreseeable flaws in the system. Later in the process might
be too late.

With that being said, don't let anyone get you down. Take con-
structive feedback and let people help you refine your vision, but
don't be dissuaded from continuing. Some of the most innovative ideas seemed completely unviable in their early stages but
proved to be game changers later on.

CREATE A COMMUNITY

Reach out to the same trusted people you sought feedback from
and turn them into followers and supporters for your campaign.
Many crowdfunding studies have shown that campaigns that are

20 to 35 percent funded within the first two weeks of launch have a much better chance of succeeding than those with zero initial backers.

This step may take a while to fully develop, but don't move on until you're sure you have enough backers to reach at least 25 percent of funding before launch. This step can really make or break a campaign.

Try social networking within communities that are interested in the type of project you're creating. If you're working on a board game, join community forums of dedicated players. If you're working on a new type of road bike, join the local biking group. It's important to promote your project outside of your immediate social circle to gain wider support.

FOLLOW SUCCESSFUL FOOTSTEPS

There are plenty of successful campaign stories on the Internet, so take the time to do your research and learn from the best. Emulate strategies that have worked for

✳ Who's your market? The most common mistake made when launching a funding campaign is forgetting to do your research.

DID YOU KNOW

Forbes named "partial purchasing" the next big thing for crowdfunding. This form of crowdfunding allows people to join forces to pitch in small amounts and purchase expensive items together.

other campaigners, and don't be afraid to reach out to the same social networks they did to garner support.

Ryan Grepper of the Coolest Cooler campaign, the highest-grossing campaign on Kickstarter as of 2015, used a combination of timing, an effective rewards system, and social connections to his backers to complete his campaign. "I feel personal responsibility to each backer that has supported me and am committed to making the Coolest Cooler live up to its name," Gepper told CNN.

He also set the bar low—he aimed for and successfully raised $50,000, unlike his first attempt, when he failed to meet his goal of $125,000. He met his goal within 36 hours of launch, creating a buzz around his project that had backers scrambling to contribute before his end date to purchase a Coolest Cooler.

There are plenty of other campaigns to learn from, such as the Pebble Watch, Bibliotheca, and the Micro 3-D Printer. Find one that you connect to, and read up!

FOCUS ON THE PRESENTATION

Your campaign page is the first and sometimes only thing a potential donor will see before deciding whether they'll give you funds; make sure it's a winner. Be sure to include appealing visuals, such as high-resolution photography, charts, and a timeline.

This is a good time to develop a prototype of the product you envision creating. Be sure to mention any experience you have creating the sort of project you hope to embark on, and share your business plan and budget. Funders want to know exactly where their money is going.

Have friends and potential supporters read your campaign draft and give you feedback. Make sure the wording is exciting and engaging to your audience.

SHOOT THAT VIDEO!

Make a video that best represents you and your project. Consider investing in a local videographer, or ask a friend with experience to help you shoot. The promotional video can have a huge impact on the success of your project.

According to Kickstarter, "projects with videos succeed at a much higher rate than those without (50 percent versus 30 percent)." That's definitely worth an investment of your time, effort, and possibly some money.

Remember to be yourself in the video. Kickstarter is a social website after all, and the campaigns also build community around their ideas. Potential donors are looking at you as well as your idea—make sure you appear competent and trustworthy, but also have fun!

Don't make the next short film—your video has 10 seconds or less to get a viewer interested, so make sure they count. Don't sacrifice important information for the sake of brevity—make sure you mention who you are and why you're interested in your project. Ask for support. Try to pitch them your rewards while you're at it—you are trying to make a sale!

SET A FUNDING GOAL

It's very important to make sure you are asking for a realistic amount of money for your project. Ask yourself how much you need to start the project, and make sure that includes the cost of issuing your rewards. Make a budget that you can share with donors so they know exactly how you will spend their funds. This is an important step, especially for platforms that only let you take home the funds if you meet this goal. Setting the bar too high might mean that even if you receive plenty of support, you may not be able to start the project.

DEVELOP YOUR REWARDS SYSTEM

Depending on the platform you choose, you'll be required (or feel highly inclined) to offer a rewards system. If you're working on a personal funding or donation-based project, feel free to move on.

A rewards system is an essential component of many crowdfunding campaigns. Rewards are how you thank donors for their contribution to your project. Develop a rewards system that is engaging to users but is also something you can realistically achieve. You have to follow through on the commitments to your contributors or you will suffer a big hit to your presentation—not to mention there is a chance of you opening your campaign up to lawsuits.

A great thing to remember is to have enough reward tiers so everyone benefits. The $1 reward on Kickstarter has proven to be a huge success. Even those strapped for cash can add $1 toward your campaign, and the reward doesn't have to be much. Successful campaigners have offered to "shout your name as [they] chase a duck," or give "a big, inviting void of nothingness. Enjoy! (Shipping included.)"

LAUNCH!

Are you ready to dedicate the next weeks or months to promoting your campaign? Make sure you've picked the right time—not only for your product, but also for yourself. It would be a shame to put that much work into preparing and then launch your project right before you take off for Costa Rica for six days. Remember: Once you hit that button, your life is the campaign.

ARE YOU READY?

Don't launch without making sure you've taken care of these points:

I. **Project Thumbnail:** Make sure you develop a good thumbnail image for your campaign. It is literally the first visual representation users will see.

II. **Project Title:** This is the only searchable text for your campaign. Make sure it adequately describes your project.

III. **Video:** You. Must. Have. A. Video.

IV. **Prelaunch Outreach:** If you don't already have 20 percent of your funding pledges down before liftoff, you might never get them. Don't miss this step.

V. **Qualifications:** Are you qualified to pull off your project? If you haven't developed the skills or can't convince your donors that you have, stop right there.

A PARTING
THOUGHT

"The amount of knowledge and talent dispersed among the human race has always outstripped our capacity to harness it. Crowdsourcing corrects that—but in doing so, it also unleashes the forces of creative destruction."

—JEFF HOWE, *CROWDSOURCING*

BIBLIOGRAPHY

"20 Best Company Facebook Pages." 20 Best Company Facebook Pages. Accessed April 12, 2015. www.inc.com/ss/20-best-company-facebook-pages#19.

"A Chat with the Cara from Catarse." My Crowdfunding Study. January 31, 2012. Accessed April 12, 2015. www.mycrowdfundingstudy.com/2012/01/31/a-chat-with-one-of-the-caras-of-catarse/.

Alois, JD. "Potato Salad Closes on Kickstarter Over $55,000." Crowdfund Insider. August 3, 2014. Accessed April 12, 2015. www.crowdfundinsider.com/2014/08/45922-potato-salad-closes-kickstarter-55000/.

Anderson, Rob. "User-Centered Innovation—Fad or the Future?" Endengene UK. Accessed April 12, 2015. www.edengene.co.uk/article/user-centred-innovation-fad-or-the-future/.

Austin, Scott. "Airbnb: From Y Combinator To $112M Funding In Three Years." Wall Street Journal. July 21, 2011. Accessed April 12, 2015. http://blogs.wsj.com/venturecapital/2011/07/25/airbnb-from-y-combinator-to-112m-funding-in-three-years/.

"Building Trust—2015 Edelman Trust Barometer." Edelman. Accessed April 12, 2015. www.edelman.com/insights/intellectual-property/2015-edelman-trust-barometer/building-trust/.

Carney, Michael. "Brian Chesky: I Lived on Cap'n McCain's and Obama O's Got AirBnB out of Debt." Pando Daily. January 10, 2013. Accessed April 12, 2015. http://pando.com/2013/01/10/brian-chesky-i-lived-on-capn-mccains-and-obama-os-got-airbnb-out-of-debt/.

Crecente, Brian. "Kickstarter Suspends Accused Airbnb Squatter's Game Project." Polygon. July 31, 2014. Accessed April 12, 2015. www.polygon.com/2014/7/31/5955597/airbnb-squatter-kickstarter-suspended.

Cunningham, Simon. "P2P Lending: What Is an Expected Return? A Survey of Industry Voices." LendingMemo. September 27, 2013. Accessed April 12, 2015. www.lendingmemo.com/peer-to-peer-lending-return/.

Dishman, Lydia. "Pebble Killed It On Kickstarter. Now What?" Fast Company. April 18, 2012. Accessed April 12, 2015. www.fastcompany.com/1834583/pebble-killed-it-kickstarter-now-what.

Elmer, Vickie. "After Disclosing Employee Salaries, Buffer Was Inundated with Resumes." Quartz. January 24, 2014. http://qz.com/169147/applications-have-doubled-to-the-company-that-discloses-its-salaries/#/h/42900,3/

BIBLIOGRAPHY

Follett, Andrew. "5 Must Read Tips for Your First Kickstarter Video." Video Brewery. Accessed April 12, 2015. www.videobrewery.com/blog/5-tips-kickstarter-video.

Garland, Russ. "Launch Angels Seeks $2M for Fund to Back Lesbian, Gay, Bisexual, Transgender Founders." Venture Capital Dispatch. July 16, 2014. Accessed April 12, 2015. http://blogs.wsj.com/venturecapital/2014/07/16/launch-angels-seeks-2m-for-fund-to-back-lesbian-gay-bisexual-transgender-founders/.

Gascoigne, Joel. "Open Salaries at Buffer: Our Transparent Formula and All Our Salaries." Buffer Open. December 19, 2013. Accessed April 12, 2015. https://open.bufferapp.com/introducing-open-salaries-at-buffer-including-our-transparent-formula-and-all-individual-salaries/.

Yu, Han, Zhiqi Shen, Chunyan Miao, and Bo An. "Challenges and Opportunities for Trust Management in Crowdsourcing." Web Intelligence and Intelligent Agent Technology (WI-IAT), 2012 IEEE/WIC/ACM International Conferences. December 2012. Vol.2, 486–93.

Hansell, Saul. "Beam It Down From the Web, Scotty." *The New York Times*. May 6, 2007. Accessed April 12, 2015. www.nytimes.com/2007/05/07/technology/07copy.html?pagewanted=1&_r=1.

Howe, Jeff. *Crowdsourcing: Why the Power of the Crowd Is Driving The Future of Business* (New York: Crown Business).

International Institute for Industrial Environmental Economics (IIIEE). (2009). "The Future Is Distributed: A Vision of Sustainable Economies." Lund: IIIEE.

Johansson, Allan, Peter Kisch, and Murat Mirata. "Distributed Eceonomies—A New Engine for Innovation." Journal of Cleaner Production 13, no. 10-11, 971-79. www.sciencedirect.com/science/article/pii/S0959652604002719.

Kamps, Haje Jan. "How a Half-million Dollar Kickstarter Project Can Crash and Burn." Medium. March 2, 2015. Accessed April 12, 2015. https://medium.com/@Haje/how-a-half-million-dollar-kickstarter-project-can-crash-and-burn-5482d7d33ee1.

Kerpen, Dave. "9 Lessons From Successful Brands on Twitter." Mashable. June 9, 2011. Accessed April 12, 2015. http://mashable.com/2011/06/09/brands-twitter-success/.

"Kickstarter Basics." Kickstarter. Accessed April 12, 2015. www.kickstarter.com/help/faq/kickstarter basics?ref=footer.

Kimball, Diana. "The Power of $1." Kickstarter. July 31, 2012. Accessed
April 12, 2015. www.kickstarter.com/blog/the-power-of-1-0.

Kovach, Steve. "Why the Guy Behind the Most Popular Smartwatch
in the World Isn't Scared of Apple." *Business Insider*. September 30,
2014. Accessed April 12, 2015. www.businessinsider.com/eric-migi-
covsky-pebble-ceo-interview-2014-9.

Lawler, Ryan. "Getaround Gets $24M in Strategic Funding to Bring Peer-
to-Peer Car Rentals to New Markets." TechCrunch. November 20, 2014.
Accessed April 12, 2015. http://techcrunch.com/2014/11/20/getar-
ound-24m/.

Learned, Andrea. "Leadership and Transparency 2015: The Social
Media Imperative." The Huffington Post. January 5, 2015. Accessed
April 12, 2015. www.huffingtonpost.com/andrea-learned/leader-
ship-and-transparen_b_6407498.html.

"Lending Club Statistics." Lending Club. Accessed April 12, 2015. www.
lendingclub.com/info/statistics.action.

Mangalindan, JP. "In Price Wars, Some Uber and Lyft Drivers Feel
The Crunch." *Fortune*. May 28, 2014. Accessed April 12, 2015. http://
fortune.com/2014/05/28/in-price-wars-some-uber-and-lyft-drivers-
feel-the-crunch/.

Martinez, Paul. "11 Things All Failed Kickstarter Projects Do Wrong."
The Comic Starter. Accessed April 12, 2015. http://thecomicstarter.
com/2014/03/15/11-things-all-failed-kickstarter-projects-do-wrong/.

McDonough, Katie. "GoFundMe Bans All Content "Relating to" Abortion—Leaves Antiabortion Campaigns Active." Salon. September 10,
2014. Accessed April 12, 2015. www.salon.com/2014/09/10/gofundme_
bans_all_content_relating_to_abortion_but_leaves_antiabortion_cam-
paigns_active/.

Medved, Jon. "Equity Crowdfunding for Dummies: How It Works & How to
Get In on the Game." VentureBeat. March 31, 2014. Accessed April 12,
2015. http://venturebeat.com/2014/03/31/equity-crowdfunding-how-
it-works-and-how-to-get-in-on-the-game/.

Miller, Jared. "TGN Interview: Elan Lee of Exploding Kittens." Tabletop
Gaming News. January 30, 2015. Accessed April 12, 2015. www.table-
topgamingnews.com/tgn-interview-elan-lee-of-exploding-kittens/.

Naughton, John. "Twitter and the Transformation of Democracy." *The
Guardian*. September 14, 2013. Accessed April 12, 2015. www.theguardian.

com/commentisfree/2013/sep/14/twitter-flotation-facebook-politics-social-network.

O'Brien, Sara Ashley. "The Coolest Kickstarter Ever Raises Over $13 Million." CNN Money. August 29, 2014. Accessed April 12, 2015. http://money.cnn.com/2014/08/29/smallbusiness/coolest-cooler-kickstarter-campaign-ends/.

Opsahl, Kurt. "Six Things You Need to Know About Facebook Connections." Electronic Frontier Foundation. May 4, 2010. Accessed April 12, 2015. www.eff.org/deeplinks/2010/05/things-you-need-know-about-facebook.

Pi, Jeanne. "The Untold Story behind Kickstarter Stats [infographic]." VentureBeat. July 17, 2012. Accessed April 12, 2015. http://venturebeat.com/2012/07/17/the-untold-story-behind-kickstarter-stats-infographic/.

"PID-Controlled Espresso Machine - Kickstarter." Update! Kickstarter. Accessed April 12, 2015. www.kickstarter.com/projects/zpmespresso/pid-controlled-espresso-machine/posts/859816.

Prive, Tanya. "The Most Common Question That New Angel Investors Ask." *Forbes*. March 11, 2014. Accessed April 12, 2015. www.forbes.com/sites/tanyaprive/2014/03/11/the-most-common-question-that-new-angel-investors-ask-2/.

Reyes, Ferdinand. "Decentralized Markets Kills E-commerce Stars: Open-Bazaar—Bitcoin Magazine." Bitcoin Magazine. November 29, 2014. Accessed April 12, 2015. https://bitcoinmagazine.com/18782/decentralized-markets-kills-e-commerce-stars-openbazaar/.

Rogowsky, Mark. "Who's Winning Right Now in the Competition between Lyft and Uber?" *Forbes*. June 10, 2014. Accessed April 12, 2015. www.forbes.com/sites/quora/2014/06/10/whos-winning-right-now-in-the-competition-between-lyft-and-uber/.

Rusli, Evelyn. "Kickstarter Project Canceled Amid Fraud Accusations." *Wall Street Journal*. November 12, 2013. Accessed April 12, 2015. http://blogs.wsj.com/digits/2013/11/12/kickstarter-project-canceled-amid-fraud-accusations/.

Russell, Kyle. "Our Four Favorite Companies from the 500 Startups Demo Day." TechCrunch. October 21, 2014. Accessed April 12, 2015. http://techcrunch.com/2014/10/21/our-four-favorite-companies-from-the-500-startups-demo-day/.

Sharrock, Justine. "Life Behind The Wheel in the New Rideshare Economy." BuzzFeed. May 8, 2013. Accessed April 12, 2015. www.buzzfeed.

com/justinesharrock/life-behind-the-wheel-in-the-new-rideshare-economy#.igr2PQzd0R.

Shaugnessy, Haydn. "Eric Von Hippel on Innovation." Innovation Management. February 21, 2011. Accessed April 12, 2015. www.innovation-management.se/2011/02/21/eric-von-hippel-on-innovation/.

"Smarty Ring." Indiegogo. March 22, 2014. Accessed April 12, 2015. www.indiegogo.com/projects/smarty-ring--4.

Smiciklas, Mark. "Social Media Explorer." Social Media Explorer Social Media Transparency Infographic Comments. January 23, 2013. Accessed April 12, 2015. www.socialmediaexplorer.com/social-media-marketing/social-media-transparency-infographic/.

"Social Networking Fact Sheet." Pew Research Centers Internet American Life Project RSS. December 27, 2013. Accessed April 12, 2015. www.pewinternet.org/fact-sheets/social-networking-fact-sheet/.

Swanner, Nate. "ZPM Drops Automated Coffee & Kickstarter Backers." SlashGear. January 14, 2015. Accessed April 12, 2015. www.slashgear.com/zpm-drops-automated-coffee-kickstarter-backers-14364665/.

"The Openness Revolution." *The Economist*. December 13, 2014. Accessed April 12, 2015. www.economist.com/news/business/21636070-multinationals-are-forced-reveal-more-about-themselves-where-should-limits.

"Top 10 Crowdfunding Sites." Crowd Funding. Accessed April 12, 2015. www.crowdfunding.com.

Ursrey, Lawton. "Before You Launch Your Crowdfunding Campaign, Read This." *Forbes*. March 18, 2014. Accessed April 12, 2015. www.forbes.com/sites/lawtonursrey/2014/03/18/before-you-launch-your-crowdfunding-campaign-read-this/2/.

Volastro, Anthony. "A New King of Kickstarter Is Crowned!" CNBC. August 27, 2014. Accessed April 12, 2015. www.cnbc.com/id/101948741.

Ward, Matt. "The 9 Habits of Highly Effective Kickstarter Campaign Rewards—Art of the Kickstart." Art of the Kickstart. September 4, 2014. Accessed April 12, 2015. http://artofthekickstart.com/the-9-habits-of-highly-effective-kickstarter-campaign-rewards/.

Wilson, Fred. "Airbnb." AVC. March 16, 2011. Accessed April 12, 2015. http://avc.com/2011/03/airbnb/.

Wortham, Jenna. "A Few Dollars at a Time, Patrons Support Artists on the Web." *The New York Times*. August 24, 2009. Accessed April 12,

2015. www.nytimes.com/2009/08/25/technology/start-ups/25kick.
html?_r=1.

"YouCaring.com Named Best Crowdfunding Platform." *Business Wire.*
May 5, 2014. Accessed April 12, 2015. www.businesswire.com/news/
home/20140505006036/en/YouCaring.com-Named-Crowdfunding-
Platform#.VSrszYu4lE6.

INDEX

CONTINUE THE
CONVERSATION

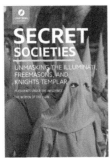

8/16

CPSIA information can be obtained at www.ICGtesting.com
Printed in the USA
BVOW11s1935310515

402410BV00003B/3/P